wicazō ša review

A Journal of Native American Studies

Editor
James Riding In, Arizona State University

Associate Editor
Amy Lonetree, University of California, Santa Cruz

Founding Editors
Elizabeth Cook-Lynn
Roger Buffalohead
Beatrice Medicine
William Willard

T0337623

Contributing Editors
Majel Boxer, Fort Lewis College
Duane Champagne, University of California, Los Angeles
Steven J. Crum, University of California, Davis
Ellen Cushman, Northeastern University
Clayton Dumont, San Francisco State University
Donald Fixico, Arizona State University
Julia Good Fox, Haskell Indian Nations University
Lawrence Gross, University of Redlands
Suzan Shown Harjo, The Morning Star Institute
Tom Holm, University of Arizona
Ted Jojola, University of New Mexico
Glenabah Martinez, University of New Mexico
Cornel Pewewardy, Portland State University
Lisa Poupart, University of Wisconsin, Green Bay
Kathryn Shanley, University of Montana
Luci Tapahonso, University of New Mexico
Laura Tohe, Arizona State University
Edward Valandra, St. Francis Mission School
Michael Yellow Bird, North Dakota State University

CONTENTS

Introduction
Brothers and Sisters in Arms

Noah Riseman

Around the world, the centenary of the First World War has accelerated what Jay Winter refers to as the memory boom of the twentieth century.[1] Nations such as Australia, Canada, and New Zealand have invested significant taxpayer dollars into commemorations of the war, continuing processes of (falsely) positioning wartime service as central to each nation's identity and development.[2] In other nations, such as the United States, it is the Second World War that has led to similar mythologies about the goodness of the nation's character and citizenry through ideas of "the Good War" and "the Greatest Generation."[3] Notwithstanding the criticisms of historians, war and conflict continue to form a central place within national collective memories. Being included within that memory is akin to being recognized as a member of the nation-state, with particular entitlements to be heard on matters of national or political importance.

As military sociologists such as Morris Janowitz argue, minorities have often viewed military service as an opportunity to demonstrate acts of citizenship and, through such acts, to point to their military service in fights for civil and political rights.[4] Scholars such as Warren Young and Ronald Krebs have debated the extent to which racial minorities may effectively leverage their position as service personnel or veterans to secure civil rights. Indeed, as both Young and Krebs argue, usually veteran or service member status alone is not enough to secure social change unless there are other catalysts within civil society that make it in the state's best interest to award civil rights to minority veterans (or, more widely, entire minority groups).[5] Even so, racial minorities, including Indigenous peoples, have for their own reasons participated in the militaries of former or current colonial powers.

I have written elsewhere about the rise of Indigenous military histories across the major Anglo settler societies of the United States, Australia, New Zealand, Canada, and South Africa. The emergence of such histories, especially since the 1990s, has aligned with national reconciliation agendas, as well as efforts among Indigenous communities to commemorate the contributions of their forebears to their country's defense.[6] This project of historicizing Indigenous military service continues around the world, exposing the complex histories of Indigenous peoples who are constantly negotiating their statuses and military service, as well as their own traditions. More recent histories have been especially interested in the intersections between military service and themes such as colonialism, gender, race relations, and martial race theory.[7] This special issue represents an extension of this new historiography, drawing scholars on Indigenous military participation from the nineteenth century until the present in the United States, Australia, New Zealand, Canada, and South Africa.

These articles derive from a conference hosted at Australian Catholic University in 2015 entitled "Brothers and Sisters in Arms: Historicising Indigenous Military Service," and they represent some of the newest directions in this growing field. Dr. Teresia Teaiwa of Victoria University of Wellington began the conference with a captivating keynote address about the historical and continuing relationship between colonialism and militarism in the Pacific, with a particular focus on Fiji. Her sophisticated arguments drew together postcolonial theory, Pacific research methodologies, and gender studies. Teresia declined the invitation to contribute an article to this collection because she needed to focus on finishing a book about Fijian women and military service. It was with great sadness that I heard Teresia that passed away in March 2017 after a brief battle with cancer. Teresia's work, and her unique approach as an oral historian using innovative and creative techniques to give voice to Pacific Islander women especially, inspired me as a historian. On behalf of all the contributors to this issue, I extend our deepest condolences to Teresia's family and dedicate this special issue to her memory.

The first article, by Mark van de Logt, returns to the American frontier to examine the role of Sahnish scouts in the wars on the Great Plains from 1865 to 1881. Van de Logt describes the relationships between the Sahnish and their white commanders, as well as their complex motivations to work for the American army in its pacification campaigns against other American Indians, namely, the Sioux. The First World War and the Cape Corps from South Africa form the subject of

Albert Grundlingh's article. Grundlingh examines colored troops and the way the South African government and military racialized their roles during and after the war, using the colored troops and their memory for various political means. Postwar experiences are also the subject of John Maynard's article, which compares two particular Indigenous rights organizations from the United States and Australia, respectively: the Mission Indian Federation and the Australian Aborigines Progressive Association. Maynard explores the activist tactics and government responses to these two organizations, drawing them into dialogue with each other and also with the First World War's legacies for Indigenous veterans and their families. R. Scott Sheffield also looks at veteran issues in his transnational article about Indigenous peoples' access to benefits after the Second World War in Canada, Australia, the United States, and New Zealand. Sheffield's analysis reveals the ways that systems supposedly designed for the welfare of all returned servicemen and servicewomen could benefit Indigenous service personnel, but only if they could overcome the structural barriers—often consequences of ongoing colonial practices—to accessing such schemes.

The last three articles examine more contemporary issues confronting Indigenous service and remembrance. My article examines the history of commemorating Aboriginal and Torres Strait Islander military service in Australia. Contrary to popular opinion, Indigenous Australians have been involved in such rituals for a long time, but it is only in recent years that they have asserted distinctly Indigenous positions within Australia's Anzac mythology, including drawing that mythology into the contentious question of commemorating the frontier wars. Maria Bargh and Quentin Whanau's article explores a new area of military experience: the private military industry. They examine the ways that constructs of Māori as "warriors" have contributed to both external perceptions and self-conceptions as friendly personnel in the private military industry who can work well with locals on overseas deployments. Finally, one of the preeminent scholars in the field of Indigenous military history, Tom Holm, revisits his landmark publication *Strong Hearts, Wounded Souls* twenty years after its publication. Holm's article, based on his conference keynote address, reflects on the process of researching and establishing support services for Native American Vietnam War veterans suffering posttraumatic stress disorder, as well as some of the lessons from that experience that can support veterans returning from Afghanistan and Iraq.

It is often said that sharing stories is part of the reconciliation process between settlers and Indigenous peoples. Military service history represents a useful lens in that process because it represents a shared history—one of patriotism, mateship, trauma, and healing. The articles in this special issue of course are only a small part of the many histories of Indigenous military service. As the centenary of the First

World War offers the opportunity to continue to reflect on the costs of wars past and present, this issue of *Wicazo Sa Review* recognizes the roles Indigenous people have played in those histories.

AUTHOR BIOGRAPHY

Noah Riseman is associate professor of history at Australian Catholic University in Melbourne. He researches the history of marginalized people in the Australian military, especially Aboriginal, Torres Strait Islander, and LGBTI people. He is the coauthor of *Defending Country: Aboriginal and Torres Strait Islander Military Service since 1945* (2016) and the author of *In Defence of Country: Life Stories of Aboriginal and Torres Strait Islander Servicemen and Women* (2016) and *Defending Whose Country? Indigenous Soldiers in the Pacific War* (2012).

NOTES

1 Jay Winter, *Remembering War: The Great War between Memory and History in the Twentieth Century* (New Haven, Conn.: Yale University Press, 2006).

2 See Marilyn Lake and Henry Reynolds, *What's Wrong with Anzac? The Militarisation of Australian History* (Sydney: University of New South Wales Press, 2010); Carolyn Holbrook, *Anzac: The Unauthorised Biography* (Sydney: NewSouth Publishing, 2014).

3 Tom Brokaw, *The Greatest Generation* (New York: Random House, 2004).

4 Morris Janowitz, "Military Institutions and Citizenship in Western Societies," *Armed Forces and Society* 2, no. 2 (1976): 185–204.

5 Warren L. Young, *Minorities and the Military: A Cross-National Study in World Perspective* (Westport, Conn.: Greenwood Press, 1982); Ronald R. Krebs, *Fighting for Rights: Military Service and the Politics of Citizenship* (Ithaca, N.Y.: Cornell University Press, 2006).

6 Noah Riseman, "The Rise of Indigenous Military History," *History Compass* 12, no. 12 (2014): 901–11.

7 For martial race theory, see Cynthia H. Enloe, *Ethnic Soldiers: State Security in Divided Societies* (Athens: University of Georgia Press, 1980), 345–70; *Police, Military and Ethnicity: Foundations of State Power* (New Brunswick, N.J.: Transaction Books, 1980); Tom Holm, "Patriots and Pawns: State Use of American Indians in the Military and the Process of Nativization in the United States," in *The State of Native America: Genocide, Colonization, and Resistance*, ed. M. Annette Jaimes (Boston: Smith End Press, 1992), 345–70.

"Whoever Makes War upon the Rees Will Be Considered Making War upon the 'Great Father'"

Sahnish Military Service on the Northern Great Plains, 1865–1881

Mark van de Logt

In the mid-1860s the Arikaras, or Sahnish, struggled against Sioux (Dakota and Lakota) incursions into their territory. After first forming an alliance with the Mandans and Hidatsas to resist Sioux expansion, Sahnish leaders White Shield and Son of Star also attempted to create a military alliance with the United States. By allowing Sahnish men to scout for the U.S. Army, White Shield and Son of Star pursued a strategy that would take the war into enemy territory and place the Sioux on the defensive.

Although racist attitudes were widespread in the U.S. Army, the Sahnish scouts gradually earned respect and appreciation for their service from regular officers and enlisted men. Among these was Lt. Col. George Armstrong Custer, who developed a close friendship with the Sahnish people. Meanwhile, realizing the danger posed by the Sahnish-U.S. military alliance, the Sioux began to target the scouts deliberately to discourage other Sahnish men from enlisting. Sadly, although the military establishment respected and appreciated the sacrifices and contributions of the scouts, the U.S. government did little to help these men after their service with the U.S. Army was over.

REACHING OUT TO THE SAHNIŠTAAKÁ (WHITE PEOPLE)

In the mid-1800s the United States and the Sioux battled each other for supremacy on the central and northern plains. The Sahnish were caught in the middle of this war. They faced a difficult decision: stay neutral, join the Sioux, or join the United States?

Joining the Sioux against the United States was not at all a logical choice for the Sahnish leadership. For nearly a century the Sahnish had suffered from attacks and harassment by the western Sioux, who had invaded Sahnish territory. According to one visitor, when they were not fighting them, the Sioux treated the Sahnish as a "kind of serf, who cultivates for them and who, as they say, takes for them the place of women."[1] Although a handful of Sioux subbands were friendly, attempts to make lasting peace agreements with the larger Sioux bands proved to be a frustrating exercise. Most of these peaceful interludes were short-lived and ended as soon as the trading season was over. Frequently, peace negotiations broke down shortly after they had started, prompting one Sahnish leader to lament that the Sioux "enter with the calumet [pipe] by one door and kill us at the other."[2] Thus, from the Sahnish perspective, long before the United States began its disgraceful record of treaty violations, the Sioux habitually broke agreements with the Sahnish people. To make matters worse, for many years the Sioux had devised a strategy to keep the Sahnish divided from their Mandan and Hidatsa neighbors and on numerous occasions intrigued to foment discord and conflict between these tribes.[3]

Considering these factors, it comes as no surprise that the Sahnish chose neutrality in the conflict between the Sioux and the United States. Frustrated by this decision, however, the Sioux attempted to bully the three tribes into taking up arms against the United States. In 1862 army captain John Patter reported that unless the United States furnished military assistance to the three tribes, the Sioux would soon "compel them to join with them against the whites."[4]

Faced with increasing pressure from the Sioux, Sahnish neešaánu' (chief) White Shield sought closer ties with the United States. In July 1864 White Shield dictated a letter to President Abraham Lincoln, reminding the government that it had promised to protect the Sahnish people in the 1851 Fort Laramie Treaty:

> We have a long time been the friends of the white man, and we will still be. . . . We are afraid of the Dakotas; they will kill us, our [women] and children, and steal our horses. We must stay in our village for fear of them. Our Great Father has promised us soldiers to help us keep the Dakotas out of our country. No help has come yet; we must wait. Has our Great Father forgotten his children? . . . Our hearts are good. We do not speak with two tongues. We like to see our white brothers come among us very much. We hear bad talk, but have no ears. When we hear good talk we have ears.[5]

With "bad talk," White Shield referred to the Sioux who were trying to pressure and talk the Sahnish into war against the United States. Unfortunately, the Great Father had "no ears" for White Shield's plea, which was immediately tabled in the vaults of the Indian Office. Indeed, the military alliance desired by White Shield would be forged not by Washington officials but rather by American military officers in the field.[6]

SAHNISH ENLISTMENT

When Gen. Alfred B. Sully's Sioux campaign arrived at Fort Berthold in August 1864, he received a warm welcome from White Shield, Son of Star, and the chiefs of the Mandans and Hidatsas. The Sioux, Sully reported, had "tried hard to get [the three tribes] to join them." They had refused, and the Sioux subsequently had forced them into a state of virtual "slavery." Sully added that the tribes "offered their services" to go out with him against the Sioux.[7]

Sully did not take up the offer for assistance that year, but when he returned in 1865, he acquired the services of Tamena Way Way or neesiRApát, better known as Bloody Knife. Sully was thoroughly impressed with his scout and suggested that they raise a company of "soldiers" from Fort Berthold, fully armed and clothed in discarded uniforms.[8] Nothing seems to have come from Sully's suggestion. Indeed, there were many factors preventing commanders from enlisting Indians: racial prejudice, the language barrier, questions about the loyalty of the scouts, and the notion that Indian scouts diminished the army's prestige. Still, the army needed help against Sitting Bull's Hunkpapa Lakotas, whose frequent attacks made the soldiers virtual prisoners in their own forts. One visitor observed that the soldiers at one post "are the worst frightened men on the Indian subject that I have ever seen."[9]

The situation changed in August 1867, when Col. Philippe Régis de Trobriand assumed command of Fort Stevenson near the Sahnish, Mandan, and Hidatsa settlement of Like a Fishhook village. Régis de Trobriand noted that many of his soldiers were so "frightened by ridiculous reports and absurd commentaries on the Indians . . . that they think more of avoiding them than of fighting them." Régis de Trobriand quickly grasped the benefits of a military alliance with the Sahnish and reached out to them. Chief White Shield assured Régis de Trobriand that his men "can fight equal numbers very well, but that their disadvantage is in their great numerical inferiority." Régis de Trobriand added that "this is what makes [the Sahnish] powerless and keeps them constantly on a cautious defensive." Perhaps Régis de Trobriand also enlisted the Sahnish scouts to prevent a possible alliance between the Arikaras with the Minneconjou Sioux, who, in the spring of 1868, had offered horses to the three tribes if they agreed to join the war against the Americans.[10]

With White Shield's approval, the first Sahnish scouts mustered in at Fort Stevenson in May 1868. Between 1868 and 1881 nearly 150 Sahnish men served as scouts on various occasions. Several Mandans and Hidatsas also joined. Every scout had his reasons for enlisting, but a desire for revenge was on almost everyone's list. For example, Red Star had lost his mother and five-year-old sister during a Sioux raid in 1862. Bloody Knife lost two brothers that same year, and another Sahnish scout named Soldier had been severely wounded in a battle with the Sioux in 1854. Others shared similar stories.[11]

Other reasons to join the army were the opportunity to leave their home at Like a Fishhook village, seek adventure, and gain war honors against their hated enemies. Monetary rewards also enticed some: "What first took the heart out of my body (made it jump with happiness)," said Soldier, "was the sight of green paper money in my hands."[12] The army also fed and housed the men and their families. Army-issued rations were particularly welcome at the end of winter, when food supplies ran low. Perhaps the most important reason to join, however, was the opportunity to defend their people against the Sioux. The army furnished the scouts with the horses and weapons with which they could engage their enemies on equal terms. In this regard, the Sahnish were similar to other Native American groups, such as the Pawnees, Crows, Apaches, Seminoles, Delawares, and many more, who fought alongside the United States against enemy tribes. Indeed, Native Americans of most nations volunteered to serve with the U.S. Army at one point or another. In these cases, too, scouts had personal and political reasons to enlist. Personal reasons included the desire to gain military honors, exact revenge, acquire horses, or earn additional income. Political reasons benefited the tribe or community as a whole. Such scouts hoped to gain better negotiating positions with the U.S. government, or, if they served against people of their own community, they may have hoped to persuade these people to give up their resistance, thus avoiding additional bloodshed.[13]

Although military service drained Like a Fishhook village of warriors, White Shield and Son of Star encouraged their men to join. They reasoned that by taking the war to the Sioux, the Sahnish enjoyed greater security at home. Perhaps they also thought (erroneously, as it turned out later) that their alliance with the army would give them greater leverage in future negotiations with the U.S. government. Perhaps just as important was the fact that the army treated the Sahnish as men and not as "children," as the agents of the Indian Office were prone to do.

During their service, the Sahnish scouts guided troops through unfamiliar terrain, carried mail and dispatches between commands, escorted hay and water details, protected railroad survey crews, policed Indian reservations, and caught and returned army deserters. During military expeditions they protected the flanks of the column, hunted meat to feed hungry troops, and spearheaded attacks against enemy encampments. The Sahnish scouts would eventually serve bravely and honorably in numerous expeditions and military campaigns, including the Yellowstone expeditions of 1872 and 1873; the Black Hills expedition of 1874; the U.S.-Canadian Border Commission expedition that same year; the ill-fated Little Bighorn campaign of 1876; the Crook and Terry follow-up campaigns, also in 1876; and the successful disarming and dismounting of the Sioux at the Standing Rock and Cheyenne River Agencies later that year.[14] Their service record is distinguished indeed.

THE SIOUX RESPONSE TO SAHNISH MILITARY SERVICE

Sahnish military service infuriated the Sioux, who began to target the scouts specifically in their campaigns. The purpose was not just to kill scouts but also to discourage other Sahnish men from enlisting.[15] Frontiersman William V. Wade observed a Sioux war party kill two Sahnish scouts escorting a teamster from Fort Lincoln. One of the Sioux involved in the attack later told Wade that they "were not looking for white men" but instead "were out to kill Rees [an alternative tribal name derived from Arickarees]."[16] Another observer wrote in 1869 that Sioux war parties were "lying around for Rees to avenge [a] scalp taken from them."[17] In June 1869 five hundred Yanktonais Sioux attacked a group of Fort Berthold hunters. While the Sioux were packing up the plunder, Chief White Shield arrived to lead a counterattack, which drove the enemy away. Despite this victory, one white observer noted that "the Rees, Gros Ventres [Hidatsas], and Mandans will get badly used this summer if they continue hostilities." He added, "It is this kind of war that is destroying the Indians faster than war with the whites."[18]

Although the Sioux tried to intimidate the Sahnish to prevent them from serving as scouts, Sitting Bull still hoped to draw the Sahnish into an alliance. When his men ran into a squad of scouts on May 17, 1868, one of the scouts, Bull Head, was thrown from his horse. Sitting Bull refused to kill Bull Head. Although one Sahnish scout later claimed that Sitting Bull spared Bull Head because they both belonged to the New Dog society, it appears that Sitting Bull, ever the statesman, still hoped to convince the Sahnish to give up their alliance with the United States.[19]

In 1873 the Hunkpapas once again attempted to persuade the Sahnish to join forces. Capt. J. P. Schindel at nearby Fort Stevenson reported that "these Berthold Indians are continually being invited by the Unkpapa Sioux (with whom they are on friendly terms) to join them in their depredations, telling them that, for being the white man's friend they are starved, while they (the Sioux) kill the whites and take what they want from them and have always plenty."[20]

Usually, however, the Sioux killed scouts without hesitation when the opportunity arose. In October 1872 a Sioux war party killed two Sahnish scouts near Fort McKeen.[21] Several others were killed later.[22] Indeed, losses that month were so high that Lt. Col. William Passamore Carlin, the commanding officer at Fort McKeen, reported that the scouts had become "rather discouraged." "I have promised them not to send them out," Carlin reported, "except with Troops, and not to expose them unnecessarily." Despite Carlin's assurances, several scouts left the service that day.[23]

The remaining scouts faced increasing danger. That same month, October 1872, Carlin received news that six hundred Sioux warriors from Grand River were on their way to "attack the 'Rees' at Fort McKeen, their plan being to show a few warriors so as to draw out the scouts and surround them with superior numbers."[24] During the attack, on November 3, the Sioux notified the commanding officer at Fort McKeen that "they did not come to fight the troops but the Rees." They added that if the troops killed any Indians, they would kill ten soldiers in return.[25] Carlin notified the Sioux agent at Grand River that he would not tolerate any hostile action against his scouts. These scouts, Carlin wrote, are "a part of this Command and any attack made on them is made on the Post." Carlin added that he had shot at the Sioux not to frighten them "but to kill them if possible and [I] shall always use whatever force I may deem necessary to punish them whenever they approach this Post with the view of attacking my Scouts or for any other hostile purpose."[26]

Heartened by the army's support, White Shield's successor, Son of Star, encouraged his men to continue their military service. In 1875 he traveled to Washington, D.C., to meet with President Ulysses S. Grant, who reportedly asked him for scouts in the upcoming war with the Sioux. Son of Star agreed to have his "boys" take part in the expedition. The next year, preparations for the 1876 campaign were under way, and many Sahnish were anxious to enlist. Red Bear, however, joined after being admonished by Son of Star to do so. Son of Star's words "touched my pride," Red Bear said later. Together with other men, Red Bear went to Tom Custer's office, where they "touched the pen." Thirty-eight Sahnish scouts served in the Little Bighorn campaign that year.[27]

ATTITUDES OF OFFICERS AND ENLISTED MEN TOWARD THE SAHNISH SCOUTS

It is difficult to reconstruct the attitudes of regularly enlisted soldiers toward the Sahnish scouts. Most soldiers simply observed the scouts from a distance and did not interact with them. Because they never established true friendships, the Sahnish remained strangers to the soldiers. In typical nineteenth-century fashion, most soldiers called the scouts' behavior "uncivilized," and they frequently referred to the scouts as "savages."[28]

Still, most soldiers valued the work of their guides. Post surgeon Dr. James M. DeWolf wrote to his wife in 1876 that he felt very safe in camp at night because "the Indian Scouts are all camped tonight outside us."[29] Lt. Charles Braden, who accompanied the scouts on the Yellowstone expedition of 1873, was impressed by their physical abilities. For example, Bloody Knife's "naked eyes . . . [were] better than ours with the glasses thrown in." Braden also enjoyed observing a Sahnish "scalp dance," although he did not think highly of the skills of Sahnish doctors.[30] Sahnish dance performances bewildered some men. "To witness their singular ceremony once is quite interesting," wrote one soldier in 1874, "but when one is kept awake half the night as a regular thing, and is expected to breakfast at 3 o'clock every morning, it loses its romance."[31] Frontier photographer Stanley J. Morrow agreed: "They don't seem to know when to drop their drumming and dancing."[32] Witnessing a Sahnish scalp dance in 1873, Pvt. Charles "Chip" Creighton, Seventh Cavalry, was scandalized by the sight of "painted, almost naked Rees." He added, "Their weird yells made my blood curdle."[33]

Other soldiers enjoyed the dances, games, and ceremonies of the scouts.[34] Lt. Hugh L. Scott, who joined the Seventh Cavalry after the Little Bighorn battle, took an almost scientific interest in them. "I lived just as they did, and allowed no custom to go unnoticed," Scott wrote. Although Scott constantly badgered his scouts to teach him, "they were always the very soul of affability, anxious to impart information wherever possible."[35]

Several civilians also observed the scouts in the field. Professor Aris B. Donaldson, a scientist with the 1874 Black Hills expedition, praised their work. "As scouts, they are invaluable," Donaldson wrote: "Where they scour the country, no ambush could be successfully laid. . . . White men could hardly equal them in the capacity of scouts." Lt. Col. George Custer, who led the 1874 expedition, also reported his satisfaction with his scouts.[36]

Although commanding officers generally appreciated the work of their scouts, tensions occasionally arose between individual enlisted men and the Sahnish. Thus, when White Shield heard a rumor of a fight between two scouts and some soldiers in 1872, he immediately traveled to Fort Buford to investigate the matter. In a letter of introduction, Indian Agent John Tappan clarified that White Shield and Son of Star wanted to ensure that their men were treated well: "They are anxious to be of service to you—and to their people and this visit is to have a friendly understanding between you and them."[37]

Despite such incidents, the Sahnish scouts continued to serve honorably and earned appreciation from officers. Lt. Col. Dan Huston, Sixth Infantry Regiment at Fort Stevenson, reported in August 1875 that the Indian scouts had "been very useful and efficient in the discharge of their duties, which consist in herding and taking care of Beef cattle, doing escort duty and acting as guides and couriers."[38] Lt. Edward Maguire, head of Custer's Corps of Engineers in 1876, wrote that the scouts "have the reputation of being very brave, and, indeed, well-known officers of the Army are willing to testify to their character in this respect."[39]

Col. Henry H. Morrow at Fort Buford appreciated the scouts because they protected his garrison and secured communication lines with department headquarters. Morrow kept his scouts happy by issuing extra rations to their families, and he also tried to secure pensions for widows of scouts who had been killed in the line of duty. At Morrow's insistence, the acting commissioner of pensions determined that "if an Indian Scout is serving with a regular organized Military Force of the U.S. and is killed while in the performance of duty, his widow will be entitled to the same benefit of the Pension Laws, as the widow of any other Enlisted man."[40]

SAHNISH VIEWS OF ARMY LIFE

Although soldiers occasionally looked down on the scouts, the reverse was true as well. While chasing the Sioux during the Yellowstone River expedition in 1873, the scouts became quite disgusted with soldiers who refused to cross the river because they could not swim. Custer, who commanded the troops, balked at Bloody Knife's suggestion that the soldiers could hang on to their horses' tails and be "towed" across. By the time the scouts had manufactured a few bull boats, the Sioux had escaped.[41]

The scouts did not have much confidence in the abilities of their regimental doctors. Even regular soldiers complained about these surgeons and often called them "butchers." Not surprisingly, the scouts preferred their own remedies and treatments over those of the white doctors.[42]

Sometimes the behavior of the enlisted men puzzled the Sahnish. When soldiers started plundering a Sioux graveyard during the Little Bighorn campaign, the scouts objected. At Bloody Knife's insistence, officers stopped the looting. One soldier later commented that all those who had looted the graves were killed at Little Bighorn. The same soldiers who considered the practice of scalping enemies to be uncivilized had no qualms about desecrating Indian graves and corpses.[43]

The Sahnish scouts often used nicknames to describe officers and men. The scouts called Gen. Alfred H. Terry One Star, Custer was Long

Hair or Hard Back-sides, and Capt. Thomas Ward Custer was Wounded Face.[44] Because of his arrogant manner and his insistence on military discipline, the scouts nicknamed Lt. Charles A. Varnum Peaked Face or Long Face. Indeed, during most of the 1876 campaign the Sahnish mostly ignored Varnum, relying instead upon their own leaders, such as Bloody Knife and Stabbed, as well as upon Custer himself.[45]

Cultural and linguistic barriers explain why scouts and regularly enlisted men kept to their own. In addition, the scouts were often too busy scouting for the army or looking after their families to establish long-term friendships. Soldiers, too, usually kept closest to their own unit.

SAHNISH RELATIONS WITH
LONG HAIR (CUSTER)

If scout relations with the officers and enlisted men were professionally distant, their relationship with Lt. Col. George Armstrong Custer was one of warmth and friendship. Although many American Indians today despise Custer (the National Congress of American Indians once labeled him the Adolf Eichmann of the nineteenth century), the Sahnish scouts considered him a true friend and ally.[46] Custer's flamboyant appearance was not the only thing that impressed the scouts, who nicknamed him Ouxčes (Long-Yellow-Hair Chief or simply Long Hair).[47] They also admired his endurance, energy, and determination, his hunting abilities, and, above all, his sincere interest in their well-being.[48] Custer looked after not only his scouts but also their families at the forts and their relatives on the reservation. In 1874 Custer asked permission from Gen. Philip H. Sheridan "to defend the Rees from the assaults of the Indians . . . as if the attacks were made on white settlers." Should enemies "attack the Rees at Berthold," he wrote, "I propose to look for their trail and follow them wherever they may be."[49]

While stationed at Fort Abraham Lincoln, Custer also tried to broker peace between the three tribes and the Sioux. Chief White Shield had complained earlier that the Sioux "will never listen to the 'Great Father' until the soldiers stick their bayonets in their ears and make them."[50] Taking White Shield's words to heart, Custer addressed the Sioux delegation. He stated that the Sahnish "are not only warm and faithful friends to the whites, but that many of their chiefs and warriors . . . have become soldiers of the 'Great Father.'" He added that "whoever makes war upon the [Sahnish] will be considered making war upon the 'Great Father' and his children."[51] In other words, Custer promised to retaliate if the Sioux broke the peace with the three tribes. Custer in fact overstepped his authority with this commitment, because it was U.S. policy not to take sides in intertribal conflicts. The exact reasons for Custer's statement are unclear. Perhaps he wanted to ensure continued loyalty of the Sahnish and their Mandan and Hidatsa neighbors for future campaigns. To be sure, to the Sahnish Custer's promise sounded like further evidence that he (and therefore the United States) was firmly on their side.

Although Custer believed that Indians in general were intellectually and culturally inferior, he nevertheless admired their "proficiency in horsemanship, personal combat, plainscraft, and hunting."[52] During the Little Bighorn campaign, newspaper reporter Mark Kellogg noted that Custer felt "much at home" among his scouts.[53] Although one could argue that Custer pretended to enjoy their company to maintain good relations with his scouts, whom he considered instrumental in satisfying his personal ambitions, it may also indicate a sincere respect for and interest in their culture. He often attended and enjoyed the dances and ceremonies of his scouts. "Custer had a heart like an Indian," said Red Star, one of the scouts. "If we ever left out one thing in our ceremonies he always suggested it to us."[54]

Because of their friendship with Custer, the scouts were not afraid to voice their displeasure with him if they felt it was warranted. During the Black Hills expedition of 1874, the scouts publicly scorned Custer for releasing a Sioux prisoner.[55] Shortly before the Little Bighorn battle, the scouts expressed their misgivings about Custer's decision to go ahead with the attack. They nevertheless rode into battle with him.[56]

During the Little Bighorn campaign, Custer often visited the scouts for supper. On several occasions he told the scouts that this would be his last Indian campaign. Custer claimed that he needed only one more battlefield victory to become the "Great Father" (the usual Sahnish term for the president) of all Indians. He promised the scouts that, once he was in office, their families would have plenty to eat "for all time to come."[57] There has been considerable debate over what Custer meant by these words. Historian Robert F. Utley, for example, argued that Custer sought a general's star. Even though Custer's exact intentions are not entirely clear, the scouts were convinced that he indeed referred to the presidency. As with the treaty negotiations with the Hunkpapas earlier, Custer was in no position to make such promises. Although it remains uncertain whether his words were poorly translated at the time (interpreter Frederick F. Gerard's interpreting skills were limited) or whether enthusiasm had carried him away, it seems oddly out of character that he would have intentionally lied to the scouts.[58]

Although some officers heaped the blame for the disaster at Little Bighorn on the scouts, the fact is that the scouts fought bravely that day.[59] Indeed, three of their best warriors, Bloody Knife, Bobtail Bull, and Little Brave, were killed in the battle, and another, Goose, was severely wounded. These heavy losses were the price for taking the war into Sioux territory. As a result of these men's sacrifices, the Sahnish people back home were safer than before because the scouts kept the

Sioux on the defensive. Therefore, even after the battle, the scouts continued to serve faithfully with the army. It is a testimony to their dedication and bravery that, although the Little Bighorn battle had shaken their confidence in the supposed invincibility of the U.S. Army, they nevertheless continued to perform dangerous duties. Undoubtedly, they concluded that despite the shocking defeat at the Little Bighorn, the United States would eventually be victorious. Subsequent events proved they were correct.

"TIWENASAAKARÍČI" (TODAY WE REMEMBER THEM): THE LEGACY OF THE SAHNISH SCOUTS

After their retirement the scouts remained proud of their service. In 1889 they joined a Fourth of July parade in Bismarck dressed in their Indian and scout regalia.[60] In August 1912 they organized a society called the United States Volunteer Indian Scouts whose purpose was "to preserve the record of their services to the Nation and to honor the memory of departed scouts by annual exercises on Memorial Day." The society also appealed to the government for pensions for the old scouts and their families. Society members composed several songs in honor of their comrades who had died at the Little Bighorn. Indeed, to many Sahnish people today, the scouts served to protect the interests of the Sahnish people rather than those of the United States. Furthermore, their strategy was successful: by serving as allies of the U.S. Army, the Sahnish scouts achieved the self-preservation of their people through the defeat of their enemies.[61]

Such efforts came with a price. Many scouts had suffered wounds or injuries during their service. Red Bear, who had enlisted in 1872 under the name Wah Nee (Handsome Elk), lost his right eye when a piece of straw lodged itself there while he was out on hay detail.[62] Several scouts, such as Ree Chief, had lost fingers, hands, and feet while serving during the cold winter months. Peter Beauchamp attributed his rheumatism to his service during the winters. Others, such as Bear's Ears and Black Calf, had been injured when they were thrown from their horses during battle. Bull Head, who had served ten years as a scout, had been severely wounded when the Sioux nearly beat him to death in 1868. Friendly fire cost Goose several fingers on his left hand. Standing Bull, who had served for five and a half years, had been shot in both legs, one arm, and the right lung and suffered greatly from these wounds later in life. Three Bears had been shot through the neck. Several, such as Young Bear, still carried bullets or bullet fragments in their bodies after their service.[63]

Unfortunately, many veterans felt that the federal government failed to recognize their sacrifices. In 1890 Agent Jonathan S. Murphy noted that the Sahnish were becoming increasingly bitter and impatient with the government. One Sahnish told Murphy that the government was treating its former enemies better than its lifelong friends: "It is a fact by no means to the credit of the Government that the Gros Ventres, Mandans, and Arickarees have been less regarded by it than any other tribes, and this notwithstanding that they have always deserved better at its hands than almost any tribe on the continent."[64]

Similarly frustrating were the scouts' attempts to get pensions for their service. Both President Grant and Lieutenant Colonel Custer had promised the scouts that they would be taken care of after retiring from military service. Sadly, few of the scouts ever received pensions. In 1891 Agent Murphy wrote a long letter on behalf of the veterans to the secretary of the interior. Murphy stated that the scouts had served honorably and deserved a pension as much as, if not more than, the white soldiers who had served: "It would appear no more than just for the Government to recognize such commendable conduct on the part of Indians as well as on behalf of white soldiers."[65]

In 1910 Enemy Heart, Red Bear, and Alfred "Bear" Young Hawk traveled to Washington, D.C., to draw attention to the scouts. Congressman Louis B. Hanna picked up their cause and submitted the scouts' discharge papers with the Pension Office. Unfortunately, the papers were lost in the shuffle from one office to the next. Most of the Sahnish veterans gave up or died before ever receiving a pension. Only a handful of scouts were successful. For example, Red Star's application was finally honored on July 24, 1939, yet Red Star had passed away less than two months before.[66]

Even though the government proved to be a source of frustration for the retired scouts, they continued to treasure their service with the U.S. Army and their friendship with George Armstrong Custer in particular. In a letter to Custer's widow, Libbie, in 1917, Melvin Gilmore, curator at the State Historical Society Museum in Bismarck, North Dakota, described the reaction of two old scouts who saw a picture of their old commander while visiting the museum:

> Some months ago two of these old men and their wives were in the museum. I called the attention of one of them to the portrait of Gen. Custer hanging on the wall. The other man was in another part of the museum at the time. The first one called him and told him in the Arikara language what I had shown him. The second man came over to see, and as soon as he looked on the portrait of his old commander he took off his hat and stood and looked at the portrait a long time respectfully and told the other people in the Arikara language some of his recollections of the general.[67]

The veterans also composed a song to honor Custer, which they sang during a Memorial Day ceremony in 1917.[68] This song, which is often sung in conjunction with honor songs to Bloody Knife, Bobtailed Bull, and Little Brave, is known as the "Custer Song." It has since become a popular Sahnish song. The song tells of how much they missed him:

> wetikiiwaato'
> wetikiiwaato', wetikiiwaato'
> uxčes wetanuhčitA nikoowaato
>
> (Now I'm lonesome
> I'm lonesome, I'm lonesome.
> Custer, he's the cause of my being lonely.)

Although Custer's popular image has declined over the past century, the Sahnish people continue to honor him. To them, Custer was not an agent of American imperialism and colonialism but a true friend and brother-in-arms with the heart of a Sahnish. The "Custer Song" in fact celebrates their long-standing ties with the U.S. Army.

To modern-day Sahnish, the scouts were the first true Sahnish American patriots, and their military service has since inspired others to serve in the different branches of the military as well. Indeed, twentieth-century military service allowed the Sahnish to revitalize traditional martial practices (including war and victory dances) and develop new organizations (such as an American Legion post named after First World War hero Joseph Younghawk), as well as new celebrations. In this form, the Sahnish "nativized" or "syncretized" military service, cloaking it in American Indian terms. The emphasis here was on the "maintenance of Indian identity and the individual's sense of peoplehood." In addition, such practices often helped returning veterans fight traumatic war experiences.[69] Present-day Sahnish credit the scouts as the originators of many of these newer traditions.

CONCLUSION

In her keynote address on Fijian military service, which opened the "Brothers and Sisters in Arms" conference in Melbourne, Teresia Teaiwa suggested that military service was simply another way in which native peoples were integrated into the colonial power's superstructure. As Teaiwa pointed out, Fijian agency was limited not only because it was driven by poverty but also because military service allowed only a limited degree of upward social mobility.

Teaiwa's observation seems to apply as well to the situation in which the Sahnish found themselves in the 1860s. Confined to an ever-shrinking land base, faced with a declining population as a result of diseases and shrinking food resources, and caught in the geopolitical power struggle between the United States and the Sioux, the impoverished Sahnish had to make a strategic decision. Their choice was either to submit to the Sioux or to join the United States. Chiefs White Shield and Son of Star chose the latter.

The Sahnish today are proud of the military service of their scout ancestors for two reasons. First (and foremost), the scouts served to defend the interests of the Sahnish people, not those of the U.S. government. The scouts successfully placed their enemies on the defensive, thus keeping the people at home safe. Second, as allies of the United States, the Sahnish achieved their strategic goal of self-preservation. The Sahnish, then and now, did not regard the scouts as "tools" of American imperialism but rather as allies of the United States. While it is true that the United States ultimately proved to be a fickle and unreliable friend, the Sahnish had every reason to believe that the Sioux would not have treated them any better; instead, the Sioux would have treated the Sahnish worse. For decades the Sahnish had suffered from attacks and harassment by the Sioux. Attempts to make peace had been frustrated time and again. The Sioux had schemed to prevent an alliance between the Sahnish, Mandans, and Hidatsas by fomenting dissent and conflict between these tribes. Finally, when the U.S.–Sioux conflict broke out, the Sioux attempted to force the Sahnish into an alliance through fear and intimidation.

For the U.S. Army, the enlistment of the Sahnish scouts was not a matter of policy to divide and conquer American Indians or exploit ethnic and intertribal tensions.[70] It was rather a matter of practicality dictated by circumstances in the field. Sahnish scouts were attractive allies for the U.S. Army because they could be discharged when they were no longer needed, they were accustomed to long days in the field, and they did not require extensive training. Additionally, most of them were battle hardened. Similarly, enlistment was not designed to integrate Sahnish men into the American mainstream. Such a policy did not occur until the Spanish-American War and First World War. In the 1860s and 1870s, economic and tactical considerations took precedence over integration and assimilation. The dichotomy of tribal versus "national" interests continues to attract the attention of scholars to this day. Apart from satisfying personal needs and ambitions, what, scholars ask, takes precedence when Native American men and women enlist in the U.S. military nowadays? Do tribal considerations (protecting tribal interests, etc.) take precedence over those of the United States as a whole? In the case of the Sahnish servicemen and servicewomen, all of these factors are of importance, but the inspirational legacy of their scout ancestors is equally indisputable.[71]

At the personal level, the benefits of military service were limited. Their struggles for pensions illustrate that the scouts were treated poorly by the United States after their service. Still, officers such as Col. Henry Morrow sought to secure the same rights for scouts that were granted to regularly enlisted men, and George Custer on various occasions secured bonuses for scouts who had rendered especially valuable services. More importantly, however, the strategy pursued by the Sahnish chiefs had the desired effect of forcing the Sioux on the defensive and thus creating greater security for Sahnish family members at home.

There were, however, important distinctions between colonial institutions in the treatment of the scouts. Attitudes differed greatly between the War Department and the Interior Department. Although both departments were paternalistic, they were paternalistic to different degrees. The army considered the Sahnish scouts as allies and appreciated the contributions they made to the military's efficiency. The army treated Sahnish soldiers more equally (although not entirely as equals). For example, Sahnish scouts were entitled to the same rights and benefits as regularly enlisted soldiers, although government bureaucrats eventually put up many hurdles for Sahnish veterans seeking pensions. Military commanders such as Sully, Régis de Trobriand, Carlin, and Custer not only considered the Sahnish scouts as indispensable but even extended the army's protection to their relatives on the reservation. Although one might view such actions merely as political expediency to ensure the continued loyalty of the Sahnish, they actually indicate a true appreciation of the contributions made by the scouts.

The Interior Department, in contrast, never treated the Sahnish as allies; instead, it treated them as "children" or "subjects." Indeed, the Interior Department was reluctant to share its authority over American Indians with the War Department. As soon as the Indian Wars were over, Interior Department bureaucrats immediately reassumed control over the returning scouts by treating them as "dependents."

Although poverty was a major reason for Sahnish individuals to enlist in the U.S. Army and opportunities for upward social mobility for scouts were limited, the Sahnish did not lack agency. First, they sought an alliance with the United States not because of American imperialism but because of Sioux imperialism. Next, the alliance paid off strategic rewards by forcing the Sioux on the defensive. Finally, the Sahnish scouts found army life more rewarding and liberating than serving paternalistic agents on the reservation. Indeed, whereas the Sioux treated the Sahnish as "women" and Indian agents viewed them as "children," the army treated them as *men*. To the Sahnish scouts, then, American officers such as George Armstrong Custer, as well as other officers and enlisted, were true brothers-in-arms.

Mark van de Logt is assistant professor of history at Texas A&M University at Qatar. He specializes in Plains Indian history and culture, particularly Pawnee and Arikara. He is the author of *War Party in Blue: Pawnee Scouts in the U.S. Army* (2010). He has published extensively on Native American topics in scholarly journals, including *Journal of Military History* and *American Indian Quarterly*. His recent book project, *Monsters of Contact: Historical Traumas in Caddoan Oral Traditions*, is forthcoming.

NOTES

1 Annie Heloise Abel, *Tabeau's Narrative of Loisel's Expedition to the Upper Missouri* (Norman: University of Oklahoma Press, 1968), 130.

2 Douglas R. Parks, ed., "A Fur Trader among the Arikara Indians: Jean Baptiste Truteau's Journal and Description of the Upper Missouri, 1794–1796," manuscript, American Indian Studies Research Institute, Indiana University, Bloomington, n.p.

3 Abel, *Tabeau's Narrative*, 129, 132–33. For Arikara relations with the Mandans and Hidatsas, see Roger Nichols, "The Arikara Indians and the Missouri River Trade: A Quest for Survival," *Great Plains Quarterly* 2, no. 2 (1982): 77–93.

4 Capt. John Patter to Brig. Gen. Blunt, Department of Kansas, Fort Leavenworth, Kansas, July 21, 1862, National Archives, RG 393, Fort Randall, Letters Sent, vol. 16, n.p. See also Capt. W. J. Rankin to Capt. R. Torrey, December 2, 1866, National Archives and Records Administration (hereafter NARA), RG 393, Letters Received, Fort Rice, Dakota Territory, 1872–78, n.p.

5 Mahlon Wilkinson to Newton Edmunds, August 31, 1864, in *Annual Report of the Commissioner of Indian Affairs* (hereafter *ARCIA*), 1864, H. Ex. Doc., 38th Cong., 2nd sess. (Washington, D.C.: Government Printing Office,

1864), 407–8, http://digicoll.library.wisc.edu/cgi-bin/History/History-idx?type=turn&entity=History.AnnRep64.p0266&id=History.AnnRep64&isize=M.

6 See Paul N. Beck, *Columns of Vengeance: Soldiers, Sioux, and the Punitive Expeditions, 1863–1864* (Norman: University of Oklahoma Press, 2013).

7 Alfred Sully to Assistant Adjutant General's office (hereafter AAG), Department of the Northwest, August 29, 1864, in *War of the Rebellion*, series 1, vol. 41, pt. 1 (Washington, D.C.: Government Printing Office, 1893), 150–51.

8 Alfred Sully to AAG, Department of the Northwest, August 29, 1864, in *War of the Rebellion*, series 1, vol. 48, pt. 2 (Washington, D.C.: Government Printing Office, 1893), 1181, 1186.

9 Thomas W. Dunlay, *Wolves for the Blue Soldiers: Indian Scouts and Auxiliaries with the United States Army, 1860–90* (Lincoln: University of Nebraska Press, 1982), 44–45; Francis B. Robertson, "'We Are Going to Have a Big Sioux War': Colonel David S. Stanley's Yellowstone Expedition, 1872," *Montana: The Magazine of Western History* 34, no. 4 (1984): 14.

10 Lucile M. Kane, ed., *Military Life in Dakota: The Journal of Philippe Regis de Trobriand* (Lincoln: University

of Nebraska Press, 1982), 60, 67, 95, 264.

11 Orin G. Libby, ed., *The Arikara Narrative of Custer's Campaign and the Battle of the Little Bighorn* (Norman: University of Oklahoma Press, 1998), 41–46, 186, 195; Ben Innis, *Bloody Knife! Custer's Favorite Scout* (Fort Collins, Colo.: Old Army Press, 1973), 28–31.

12 Libby, *Arikara Narrative,* 46.

13 Ibid., 52, 186, 195, 200; Dunlay, *Wolves for the Blue Soldiers,* 11–24; David D. Smits, "Fighting Fire with Fire: The Frontier Army's Use of Indian Scouts and Allies in the Trans-Mississippi Campaigns, 1860–1890," *American Indian Culture and Research Journal* 22 (1998): 73–116.

14 For more information on these campaigns, see Robert F. Utley, *Frontier Regulars: The United States Army and the Indian, 1866–1891* (Lincoln: University of Nebraska Press, 1984).

15 In 1862 the Sioux also murdered Hunkpapa chief Bear's Rib for refusing to join the resisting Sioux. Report of Capt. John Patter to Brig. Gen. Blunt, July 21, 1862, NARA, RG 393, Fort Randall, Letters Sent, vol. 16.

16 William V. Wade Papers, State Historical Society of North Dakota, Small Manuscripts Collection, MS 20038, Bismarck, N.D., pp. 12–13.

17 John V. Bean to his mother, May 4, 1869, John Victor Bean Papers, State Historical Society of North Dakota, Bismarck.

18 John V. Bean to his mother, June 15, 1869, Bean Papers.

19 Libby, *Arikara Narrative,* 46–48; Kane, *Military Life in Dakota,* 283–84.

20 Capt. J. P. Schindel to AAG, Department of Dakota, June 1, 1873, NARA, RG 393, Letters Sent,

Fort Stevenson, 1871–76, vol. 1, p. 266, no. 123.

21 Lt. Daniel H. Brush to Col. David S. Stanley, October 14, 1872, NARA, RG 393, Field Records / Yellowstone Expedition 1872–73, Letters Received, box 1. See also Lt. Col. W. P. Carlin, Fort McKeen, to Maj. O. D. Greene, AAG, Department of Dakota, October 15, 1872, NARA, RG 393, Letters Sent, Fort A. Lincoln, vol. 11, June 1872–August 1873.

22 Libby, *The Arikara Narratives,* 188–89.

23 Lt. Col. W. P. Carlin, Fort McKeen, to the commander of the U.S. Troops with the NPRR surveying party, October 16, 1872, NARA, RG 393, Letters Received, Fort A. Lincoln, vol. 11, June 1872–August 1873.

24 Capt. Edward Collins to Lt. Col. W. P. Carlin, October 23, 1872, NARA, RG 393, Letters Received, Fort Rice, Dakota Territory, 1872–73.

25 Lt. Col. W. P. Carlin to Maj. O. D. Greene, November 4, 1872, NARA, RG 393, Letters Sent, Fort A. Lincoln, vol. 11, June 1872–August 1873; see also RG 75, Office of Indian Affairs, Letters Received, Dakota Superintendency, 1872 W612, M234, roll 252:410–15.

26 Lt. Col. W. P. Carlin to Commanding Officer, Grand River, Dakota Territory, November 7, 1872, NARA, RG 393, Letters Sent, Fort A. Lincoln, vol. 11, June 1872–August 1873.

27 Libby, *Arikara Narrative,* 40, 52.

28 John E. Cox, *Five Years in the United States Army* (New York: Sol Lewis, 1973), 101; Daniel O. Magnussen, ed., *Peter Thompson's Narrative of the Little Bighorn Campaign, 1876* (Glendale, Calif.: Arthur H. Clark, 1974), 61.

29 Edward S. Luce, ed., "The Diary and Letters of Dr. James M. DeWolf, Acting Assistant Surgeon, U.S. Army: His Record of the Sioux Expedition of 1876 as Kept until His Death," *North Dakota History* 25, nos. 2–3 (1958): 67, 73.

30 John M. Carroll, ed., *The Yellowstone Expedition of 1873* (Mattituck, N.Y.: J. M. Carroll and Company, 1986), 52, 58–59, 63–65.

31 Herbert Krause and Gary D. Olson, eds., *Prelude to Glory: A Newspaper Accounting of Custer's 1874 Expedition to the Black Hills* (Sioux Falls, S.D.: Brevet Press, 1974), 106.

32 Stanley J. Morrow, letter, August 14, 1870, quoted in *Frontier Photographer: Stanley J. Morrow's Dakota Years*, by Wesley R. Hurt and William E. Lass (n.p.: University of South Dakota and University of Nebraska Press, 1956), 25–26.

33 Usher L. Burdick, ed., *The Army Life of Charles "Chip" Creighton* (Paris, Md.: National Reform Associates, 1937), 10. Scalp dances were dances in which the Sahnish celebrated a victory over their enemies. The scalps (although other body parts could also be used) were paraded around on poles in celebration. When the dances were performed at home, female relatives of the victorious men were entitled to dress up in war regalia and carry the poles in honor of their victorious husbands or relatives. In addition, the Sahnish also had a version of the Pawnee New Fire Ceremony, a religious ceremony that revitalized the people. During this ceremony pieces of enemy scalps were burned in sacrifice to the sacred powers. Mark van de Logt, "'The Powers of the Heavens Shall Eat of My Smoke': The Significance of Scalping in Pawnee Warfare," *Journal of Military History* 72 (January 2008): 85–87.

34 John M. Carroll and Lawrence A. Frost, *Private Theodore Ewert's Diary of the Black Hills Expedition of 1874* (Piscataway, N.J.: CRI Books, 1976), 65–66, 74.

35 Hugh L. Scott, *Some Memories of a Soldier* (New York: Century, 1928), 33.

36 Krause and Olson, *Prelude to Glory*, 72; Innis, *Bloody Knife*, 109.

37 Indian Agent John Tappan to Lt. Col. C. E. Gilbert, Fort Buford, January 25, 1872, NARA, RG 393, Fort Buford Document File, n.p.

38 Lt. Col. Dan Huston to AAG, Department of Dakota, August 3, 1875, NARA, RG 393, Letters Sent, Fort Stevenson, 1871–76, vol. 1, p. 430, no. 144.

39 "Annual Report of Lieutenant Edward Maguire, Corps of Engineers, for the Fiscal Year Ending June 30, 1877," in *Annual Report of the Secretary of War*, 1877, vol. 2: *Engineers*, H. Ex. Doc. 1/5, serial set 1796, 45th Cong., 2nd sess. (Washington, D.C.: Government Printing Office, 1877), 1339–40.

40 Innis, *Bloody Knife*, 63.

41 James Willard Schultz, *William Jackson, Indian Scout* (Cambridge, Mass.: Riverside Press, 1926), 110; Lawrence A. Frost, *Custer's 7th Cavalry and the Campaign of 1873* (El Segundo, Calif.: Upton & Sons, 1986), chap. 6.

42 Ernest Grafe and Paul Horsted, *Exploring with Custer: The 1874 Black Hills Expedition* (Custer, S.D.: Golden Valley Press, 2005), 21–22, 145.

43 Bruce R. Liddic and Paul Harbaugh, *Custer and Company: Walter Camp's Notes on the Custer Fight* (Lincoln: University of Nebraska Press, 1998), 108–9.

44 Mark Kellogg, "Diary, 1876," State Historical Society of North Dakota, Small Manuscripts Collection, MS 21017, Bismarck, N.D.

45 Libby, *Arikara Narrative*, 72, 84, 197–98.

46 Vine Deloria Jr., *Custer Died for Your Sins: An Indian Manifesto* (New York: Macmillan, 1969), 148.

47 Schultz, *William Jackson*, 101.

48 Elizabeth B. Custer, *Boots and Saddles: or, Life in Dakota with General Custer* (Norman: University of Oklahoma Press, 1961), 268. Elizabeth "Libbie" Bacon married George Armstrong Custer in 1864. After Custer's death at the Little Bighorn battle, she wrote several memoirs detailing her life with her husband on the plains. She carefully guarded her husband's reputation after his death. For more biographical details, see Shirley A. Leckie, *Elizabeth Bacon Custer and the Making of a Myth* (Norman: University of Oklahoma Press, 1993).

49 Lt. Col. George A. Custer to the Commanding Officer at Fort Rice, May 27, 1874, NARA, RG 393, Letters Sent, Fort A. Lincoln, vol. 14A, May 1874–January 1877, pp. 63–65, no. 578.

50 Report of John A. Burbank to Commissioner E. J. Parker, *ARCIA*, 1870, H. Ex. Doc. 1/11, serial set 1445, 41st Cong., 3rd sess. (Washington, D.C.: Government Printing Office, 1870), 673–74, http://digicoll.library.wisc.edu /cgi-bin/History/History-idx?type =turn&entity=History.AnnRep70 .p0210&id=History.AnnRep70 &isize=M.

51 Frost, *Custer's 7th Cavalry*, 128–29.

52 Custer quoted in Robert M. Utley, *Cavalier in Buckskin: George Armstrong Custer and the Western Military Frontier* (Norman: University of Oklahoma Press, 1988), 149.

53 Kellogg, "Diary, 1876," 2.

54 Libby, *Arikara Narrative*, 77.

55 Carroll and Frost, *Private Theodore Ewert's Diary*, 67; Grafe and Horsted, *Exploring with Custer*, 98.

56 See Alfred Morsette Sr., "The Custer Expedition," in *Myths and Traditions of the Arikara Indians*, ed. Douglas R. Parks (Lincoln: University of Nebraska Press, 1996), 280.

57 Libby, *Arikara Narrative*, 61–62, 74, 80–82.

58 Utley, *Cavalier in Buckskin*, 164.

59 John S. Gray, "Arikara Scouts with Custer," *North Dakota History* 35 (Spring 1968): 442–78.

60 *Word Carrier*, o.s., 18, no. 8 (1889): 17.

61 According to Sahnish tribal historian Melfine Fox Everett, the Old Scouts' Society was founded after Orin G. Libby's visit to Fort Berthold in 1912.

62 Deposition by Red Bear, August 23, 1911, at Armstrong, N.D., Red Bear pension file, RG 15.7.4, National Archives, Washington, D.C.

63 Agent Jonathan S. Murphy to U.S. Secretary of the Interior, March 1891, November 4, 1890–April 14, 1891, box 516643, RG 75, NARA, photocopy at the American Indian Studies Research Institute, Indiana University, Bloomington.

64 Jonathan S. Murphy to Commissioner of Indian Affairs, August 31, 1890, *ARCIA* (Washington, D.C.: Government Printing Office, 1890), 35, http://digicoll.library.wisc.edu /cgi-bin/History/History-idx?type =goto&id=History.AnnRep90& isize=M&submit=Go+to+page &page=35.

65 Murphy to U.S. Secretary of the Interior, March 1891.

66 Herman J. Viola, *The Little Bighorn Remembered: The Untold Indian Story of Custer's Last Stand* (New York: Times Books, 1999), 147–51.

67 Melvin R. Gilmore to Elizabeth B. Custer, September 11, 1917, photocopy at the American Indian Studies Research Institute, Indiana University, Bloomington.

68 Ibid.

69 William C. Meadows, *The Co-manche Code Talkers of World War II* (Austin: University of Texas Press, 2002), 9–13; Tom Holm, "Patriots and Pawns: State Use of American Indians in the Military and the Process of Nativization in the United States," in *The State of Native America: Genocide, Colonization, and Resistance*, ed. M. Annette Jaimes (Boston: South End Press, 1992), 358–64. Holm points out that the "nativization" of military service can have problematic consequences. Not only do Native servicemen suffer from the effects of the warrior stereotype, but they are sometimes caught in a psychological crisis of cognitive dissonance when they question the legitimacy of a military action, as was the case among many servicemen during the Vietnam War. See also Russell L. Barsh, "War and the Reconfiguring of American Indian Society," *Journal of American Studies* 35, no. 3 (2001): 371–410.

70 Cynthia Enloe, *Ethnic Soldiers: State Security in Divided Societies* (Athens: University of Georgia Press, 1980).

71 Apart from the aforementioned works on this issue by Holm, Meadows, and Enloe, see also Al Carroll, *Medicine Bags and Dog Tags: American Indian Veterans from Colonial Times to the Second Iraq War* (Lincoln: University of Nebraska Press, 2008); Tom Holm, *Strong Hearts, Wounded Souls: Native American Veterans of the Vietnam War* (Austin: University of Texas Press, 1996); P. Whitney Lackenbauer, R. Scott Sheffield, and Craig Leslie Mantle, eds., *Aboriginal Peoples and Military Participation: Canadian and International Perspectives* (Kingston, Ont.: Canadian Defence Academy Press, 2007); J. Boyd Morningstorm, *The American Indian Warrior Today: Native Americans in Modern U.S. Warfare* (Manhattan, Kans.: Sunflower University Press, 2004).

Pleading Patriots and Malleable Memories

The South African Cape Corps during the First World War (1914–1918) and Its Twentieth-Century Legacy

Albert Grundlingh

N ews of the outbreak of war in Europe prompted a surge of proempire sentiments and effusive declarations of loyalty to Britain among many colored (mixed-race) people in the Union of South Africa.[1] Orchestrating and encouraging these avowals was the African Political Organisation (APO) of Dr. Abdullah Abdurahman. The APO was the main political vehicle for colored people, and its newspaper, also by the same name, played an influential role in disseminating political ideas. The First World War initially dominated the entire content of the newspaper.[2]

Mass meetings were further occasions to provide voluble support. One such meeting in the landmark Cape Town City Hall was described as "of an enthusiastic character with the audience, which embraced practically all sections of the coloured community, almost filling the floor of the spacious hall."[3] A motion of loyalty to the British Crown was accepted with wild applause. Support for the British war effort went beyond the Cape Town epicenter, and thirty towns in the Cape countryside, as well as meetings in Johannesburg and Pretoria, weighed in with similar declarations of loyalty.[4] To add substance to these patriotic sentiments, some colored notables established a special fund to help contribute to war-related initiatives.[5]

Although the vociferous support might at face value be considered as blind, unthinking loyalty and difficult to comprehend, given the prevailing levels of discrimination against colored people in the union, it did contain its own internal logic. Underpinning the enthusiastic support was the assumption that should Britain be defeated by Germany in the war, the position of colored people might well worsen. This meant that their existing grievances had to be shelved for the greater good and to help ensure an outcome that would be in favor of Britain. Although British liberty might often be found wanting in practice, the argument at the outbreak of war was that "at present our first duty . . . is to see the war through."[6]

Closely related to this line of thinking was the optimistic expectation that once the war was won, "true British liberty and justice will prevail: not the liberty and justice we have smarted under." All men of the empire, regardless of color, had to have equal opportunities, and anything short of that would be a "sham, a mockery, a betrayal, a lie."[7] A slight variation of this theme was the explicit hope that the war would drive home the notion that not one race has a monopoly of virtues, as whites were fond of believing while assigning undesirable traits to groups other than white. "The English," reported the APO newspaper, "find that the Germans are particularly base, while the Germans find the English entirely vile." On the basis of this observation, the newspaper concluded that there were "fashions in thought and the war will make entirely old-fashioned the thought that a man with a white skin must necessarily be superior to a man with a brown skin."[8] Such aspirations, which bordered on wishful thinking at the time, nevertheless reflected the deep-seated need for societal transformation and also the way in which the war was perceived as a possible catalyst for that change.

Apart from the politics of hope, the APO benefited inadvertently from the outbreak of war inasmuch as the organization could ward off more radical changes from its own constituency, which claimed that their existing conservative approach bore no fruit, for example, petitioning authorities or arranging deputations. It was with some relief that APO leaders could then claim that wartime circumstances offered them yet another opportunity, one with a greater potential than before, as they could demonstrate their worth during a crisis. The chances of such an approach yielding political dividends were considered better than embarking on rash actions like vociferous protests, which could only be construed as disloyalty to the Crown and diminish the chances of any political gain.[9] This apart, the APO newspaper, which had been sliding into a state of dormancy and bland reporting, was given a new lease of life by the war with the ready availability of dramatic news.[10]

THE ISSUE OF PARTICIPATION IN THE WAR

Given the eager support for the British war effort, it is not surprising to find that many colored men volunteered to be part of a combatant corps.

"Everyone seems determined to do his duty," Abdurahman enthused.[11] A few men even paid their own way in order to join British regiments.[12] On the basis of this enthusiasm, the APO suggested to the government that the organization would undertake to raise a corps to fight in the war.

However, in what must have been a hammer blow to the aspirations of many colored people, Premier Louis Botha declined the offer of an armed corps. The rejection of the offer was based on article 7 of the South African Defence Act of 1912, which stipulated that the obligation to render armed service was not applicable to people who were not of "European descent." These people could, however, be used for noncombatant manual work. The article precluding the use of black and colored people in a fighting capacity could nevertheless be amended under war circumstances.[13] At the outbreak of the war, Botha was loath to do this. Politically, with the government already under stress as a result of the Boer rebellion, he thought it wise to avoid any possible further controversies. It was a position that the APO firmly rejected. Botha was accused of "declining the offer out of a weak deference to an irrational prejudice—the dislike of his burghers to see any Coloured men however civilized, participate in a war between whites."[14]

Underpinning the particular clause of the Defence Act was a set of assumptions regarding the arming of black and colored people that dated to before the Anglo-Boer War. Black people had to be kept out of conflicts between whites. The British use of about thirty thousand armed black people during the hostilities of 1899–1902 still rankled many Boers. In allowing blacks to be become involved in warfare between whites, it was argued that white prestige and status could be diminished in the eyes of black people, undermining what was regarded as the orthodox relationship between races. In addition, this line of thinking proceeded from the supposition that in allowing black and colored people to be trained in the use of firearms, they might militate against whites; weaponry could then so much easier be turned against the ruling classes in the form of an armed uprising. A further hidden danger lurked in the implied possibility that combatant wartime participation might encourage demands for greater political recognition as a reward for armed service. These reservations did not apply to unarmed assistance in the form of manual labor, which was regarded as the "natural" order of things.[15]

The policy of not arming black and colored people so resolutely proclaimed in August 1914 was, however, completely reversed in late 1915 when the government decided that an armed colored corps should be recruited for campaigning in East Africa against the Germans. How is this turnaround to be explained? One consideration was that the Boer rebellion was by then suppressed and no longer a factor in political calculations. This development, though, was not an overriding concern; there were other justifications and considerations.

Gen. Jan Smuts, as officer commanding of the South African Forces in East Africa, sought in Parliament to invoke the historical record by claiming that the decision to utilize colored troops was not really a drastic departure from past practices, as in colonial times colored troops were involved in nineteenth-century warfare. It was therefore not a "novel procedure," he argued: "In almost all the campaigns waged against the natives it has been the policy of the Imperial Government and the Colonial Government to enlist coloured people to take part in the campaigns waged during the last 100 years against the natives in the Cape."[16] Technically, Smuts was correct: colored soldiers, known as "pandours," were used in a fruitless attempt to defend the British in 1795 and subsequently throughout the nineteenth century. Grouped together in a successive assortment of military units such as the Cape Regiment, the Cape Corps, and the Cape Mounted Rifles, coloreds were regularly used in the various frontier wars against the Xhosa.[17]

While Smuts's history could not be faulted, politically it was nothing more than a clever ploy to disguise more pressing reasons for seeking to enroll coloreds for armed service in East Africa. In private letters he revealed that Germans fought with black troops called "askaris," which justified the South African use of colored troops. But an issue of greater importance for Smuts was climatic conditions in East Africa and the fact that malaria had a decimating effect on white troops. East Africa, he argued, "was not a country into which to bring a force of white men and coloureds would be admirably suited for campaigning under the conditions of hot climate and bush country which obtain in East Africa."[18] Why he came to the conclusion that colored troops would be more immune to conditions remained unexplained. The strange logic can perhaps only be understood if it is seen in the common assumption of biological determinism of the early twentieth century held by many members of the white elite. This notion proceeded from the false assumption that certain races were inherently more immune than others to certain diseases.[19]

It was under the sway of such perverse reasoning that the government allowed colored people to participate in an armed capacity in the war. The decision was not primarily taken as a gesture of understanding or even an acknowledgment of the desire of colored people to assist in the war but rather as a result of wrongheaded if not cynical considerations. Colored people, however, did not generally know this at the time; had they known, colored support for the war effort might have vanished. As it turned out, despite the earlier slight of not being allowed to participate initially, the APO welcomed this change of direction in 1915. It was regarded as an important breakthrough that "the Cape Coloured men are recognised as willing to shed their blood for freedom as any other members of the British empire."[20] Symbolically, being allowed to participate in the war also implied that coloreds were on par in terms of equal citizenship.

RECRUITMENT

Although there was considerable excitement at the prospect of a fighting colored corps, the word still had to be spread, and formal recruiting had to proceed. In Cape Town and farther afield, recruitment drives were launched in 1915 with much military fanfare: bands, street parades, patriotic speeches at specially arranged meetings and bioscopes (traveling movie theaters), press notices, and stirring posters.[21] In towns where there was often little else offered in terms of entertainment, recruiting marches were popular attractions. These took the form of a march accompanied by a military band to prominent places, the observation of a midday pause, and the sounding of the "Last Post." Many colored people attended these performances, and it was reported that "on all occasions opportunities were seized to gain recruits and to put forward the cause of the Allies for civilization and humanity."[22] These drives had the desired effect. A. J. B. Desmore, a member of the Cape Corps, later recalled, "If nothing else stirred the heart to patriotism, and roused the indifferent to action, these patriotic demonstrations were most successful."[23] Recruiting propaganda was replete with patriotic notions, primarily invoking loyalty to the British Empire and second to the Union of South Africa. The call to arms was construed as being a major privilege and a form of recognition: "Today the Empire needs us. What nobler duty is there than to respond to the call of your King and Country."[24]

The recruitment campaign, which generally proceeded smoothly, did, however, experience some setbacks with regard to the conditions under which recruits were allowed to enroll. Only those with no dependents allowed to join, whereas white married men were inducted and received a separation allowance. This was, not surprisingly, considered unfair. As there were few colored men of military age without dependents, it was argued that if this regulation had to be adhered to, the whole venture should be scrapped. What a "sad spectacle," it was reported, "to see fine strapping fellows turned away for the sake of a few shillings extra."[25] At the risk of imperiling the enterprise, the stipulation was waived after appeals were made to the authorities and colored soldiers were placed on the same financial footing as their white counterparts.[26]

Recruits had to undergo strict medical and physical tests to ensure that they had the potential to become efficient soldiers on active service. Only one in four recruits was selected. Those who did not meet the requirements, which included dental examinations, had to return home. The chosen ones who remained were described in glowing terms by a white officer, but not without a hint of patronizing prejudice. He noted that these were "fine specimens of brawny manhood. So splendidly developed were many of them that it might have been a parade of prize fighters[,] and ugly in physiognomy as many of them undoubtedly were, their smiles revealed dentures that many a woman would have sacrificed a good deal to call her own."[27]

Desmore provided a tantalizing glimpse of the composition of the corps: "The bulk form the labouring class of South Africa . . . mainly as farm labourers and, in a lesser degree, in skilled trades in the towns. Forming part of the labouring class they have a very robust physique, they have perseverance and a power of endurance. . . . [M]arked cheerfulness under extreme circumstances makes them natural soldiers."[28] Many of these men would have been from the Cape countryside and some from Johannesburg and Pretoria. While the recruitment drive emanated from Cape Town, the city did not seem to have provided the majority of recruits. Nevertheless, wherever these men hailed from, the available evidence suggests that amidst the general war fervor, patriotic imperial considerations, rather than more local enthusiasms of being allowed to fight for South Africa, laced with a certain sense of touristic curiosity, were the main motives for propelling men into the corps.[29] There were exceptions, though. Some later claimed that they had joined because of material inducements such as promises of free land after the war or because they would automatically gain voting rights and be placed on par with whites.[30]

Intermittent recruiting during the war for the replenishment of the corps meant that, in total, eight thousand colored men were recruited to the Cape Corps. There were, however, also nonfighting colored units who were enrolled to do manual labor in France, namely, the Cape Coloured Regiment (CCLR) and the Cape Auxiliary Horse Transport Company (CAHTC). In total, 4,482 men found their way into these outfits.[31] Although these units were sent to the European front, their noncombatant status counted against them, and, given the prevailing war fervor of the time, both whites and the home colored communities regarded them as less glamorous and of lower status than the armed Cape Corps.[32]

WAR SERVICE

After an initial period of training, the first batch of recruits of the Cape Corps was dispatched to East Africa. On February 9, 1916, they boarded the *Armadale Castle* for Mombasa. An officer poignantly sketched the scene of departure: "Many a mother strained with tears of pride in her eyes to get a glimpse of her son; many a young coloured woman who had a very particular interest in her newly made soldier friend, moved in the crowd in the hope of a last farewell." Overall, he was very taken with what he witnessed: "With the band playing martial airs—and the sun shining upon a sea of helmets and dark skinned faces and flashing upon the trappings of the uniform, it was difficult to believe that these were the same men, who only a few months before had come to enlist at the City Hall, many ill-clad and anything but smart."[33] In East Africa the corps was first used at base camps and then assigned to the supply lines, but in time they were transferred to the battlefront. Hostilities in East Africa developed into a guerilla war that necessitated long marches over difficult terrain in an attempt to corner the evasive German forces. The corps was involved in several armed clashes; thirty-two men were killed in the field, and ninety-four were wounded.[34]

A more significant threat to life, however, was the conditions under which they had to fight. Of all the South African units in East Africa, the Cape Corps was stationed for the longest period during the rainy season in the unhealthy swampy marshland close to the Rufiji River. Blackwater fever, dysentery, and malaria were rife. In total, 126 men succumbed to disease. The corps had one of the highest malaria death rates of 8.66 per 1,000. Its extended stay of twenty-two months in East Africa added to the loss of life.[35]

During the campaign, Smuts was exceptionally hesitant to risk the lives of white troops in direct confrontation with the Germans, and this also led some officials to criticize the way in which he conducted the war.[36] Moreover, the deployment of the Cape Corps in the worst disease-ridden areas of East Africa has to be seen in conjunction with Smuts's earlier peculiar view, as noted, that colored troops were presumed to be more resistant to malaria than whites—not to mention the blatant prioritization of white lives over black or colored. This false assumption, deliberate or otherwise, helps to explain the extraordinary losses of the Cape Corps in East Africa.

News of events in East Africa surfaced in the union and elicited a sharp response. In Johannesburg the local branch of the APO wrote to Governor-General Sydney Buxton, making what they considered an obvious point: "Where men irrespective of caste, colour or creed, are fighting for their King and Country on the common field—, the Government should know one and only one policy alone." Consequently they continued, "the policy—of assigning to—coloured troops areas regarded as dangerous to local white troops, is contrary to all the spirit of sacrifice and determination with which many sections of Her Majesty's subjects have responded to the call of their King and Country."[37] As far as could be ascertained, Buxton did not respond, and it took a while for colored troops to be removed from the unhealthy areas.

Upon the return of the corps to the union, the men were granted a period of rest in Kimberley. During this period, all members had to undergo blood tests for malaria, and some were hospitalized. A sufficient number of fit men, augmented by new recruits, could be mobilized for one battalion to fight against the Turks, Germany's allies in Palestine. In April 1918 they embarked from Durban, had specialized training in Egypt, and then departed for the front in Palestine.

The men were to form part of Gen. E. Allenby's army and were involved in what turned out to be final mopping-up operations against the Turks. The high point of their expedition was to drive the Turks from what was known as Square Hill on September 19, 1918, with the loss of only one wounded and one member killed against the capture of 181 Turks. The following day, though, in an attempt to inflict further harm on the Turks, they met with unexpected stiff opposition. Of the four hundred men who participated in the attack, the corps lost forty-four killed and ninety-five wounded. Despite this setback, General Allenby had the highest regard for the corps. They "fought with the utmost bravery and rendered splendid service," he reported.[38] The men of the Cape Corps knew they had signed up for active combat, but of course they could not know precisely how battles would end. The pluck of the men in Palestine was destined to become part of Cape Corps tradition, with Square Hill in particular as a decisive battle to be remembered for generations to come. An ordinary member, A. Kammies, recalled more prosaically: "We fought hard, but one did not really have a choice; once you were in a battle you had to fight else the enemy can kill one so much easier."[39]

DEMOBILIZATION

Many units of the Cape Corps were demobilized from Kimberley in the northern Cape. A suitable military base for the corps had been a long-standing quandary for the Defence Force authorities. Initially, it was thought that Cape Town would be a logical choice, but disciplinary problems brought on by the easy manner in which liquor could be obtained, as well as the ready availability of prostitutes, which led to absenteeism, forced a reevaluation.[40] Several up-country towns were considered, but there was a concern to avoid predominantly Afrikaans-speaking places where "colour prejudice is very strong."[41] Eventually, Kimberley was decided upon, since it had a good proportion of English-speaking loyalists who, so it was argued, would be more tolerant. In addition, De Beers was prepared to provide a suitable campsite.[42]

In the event, Kimberley also proved to be problematic. Over the Christmas season of 1917 some recent returnees from East Africa were given leave to visit the town. They were less than welcomed. Christmas cheer seems to have passed some local whites by, and they objected to the presence of colored soldiers in town. On Christmas Eve the situation quickly got out of hand, and unseemly street fights ensued as whites and coloreds weighed into each other with gusto. The following day close to three hundred white men, armed with knobkerries, iron pipes, chains, and a few rifles, patrolled a tense Kimberley. After troops had stones thrown at them, a fracas developed in which thirty people were injured. When word reached the camps that corps members were once again under attack, it was only with great difficulty that the remaining men in the camp could be restrained from breaking out to assist their comrades. A troubled local commissioner of police reported that "the situation is critical and so long as the colored troops are left in Kimberley, there will be friction."[43]

Despite being a transparently one-sided view, the idea that the colored men were the source of the problem in Kimberley prevailed for a while. Over what was supposed to be the festive season, the military authorities removed the corps from the vicinity of the town, and they decamped into the veld until white antipathies in town were considered to be less volatile.[44] The unedifying situation was ironic indeed and clearly a case of blaming the victims instead of the perpetrators. This happened despite the fact that the military authorities realized that the troops were not the prime instigators. "Gross insults were being hurled at both officers and men of the Cape Corps," their commanding officer testified, and he described those who were guilty of such behavior as "larrikins and hooligans." On their part, the troops "as a general rule, have shown great forbearance and have behaved in an exemplary manner, and it was only when they found that their comrades were being seriously injured that they retaliated."[45]

Even the conclusion of hostilities in Europe in November 1918 did not mean the end of local antagonisms in Kimberley. To his dismay, Brig. Gen. J. J. Collyer, acting secretary of defense, was informed that with the ceremonial festivities associated with the declaration of peace, "the unjustifiable and disgraceful behaviour of the white larrikins of Kimberley towards the Cape Corps soldiers continues. As the Cape Corps was marching down the street, one of these monstrosities stepped from the curb and hit a Cape Corps soldier on the jaw and disappeared." This kind of behavior persisted during the proceedings, and the anomaly of the situation was not lost on Collyer: "While the Mayor was complimenting the corps on their behaviour in the field which had helped to bring about the very occasion which was being celebrated, the hooligan element was busy insulting and molesting the Cape Corps men in the ranks on the outskirts of the meeting."[46]

The events at Kimberley came somewhat as a surprise to the authorities, as the city was regarded as a white English-speaking loyalist bulwark, consisting mainly of the South African Party or Unionist supporters, with Afrikaans National Party adherents a decided minority. Yet it was precisely from the English quarter—the part supposedly more prowar and tolerant toward colored troops—that the protests and dissatisfaction emanated.[47] At the root of this was obvious racism, but the war inadvertently acted as a catalyst for such behavior.

On their return, colored troops were accused of "not knowing their place" because of their contribution to the war effort.[48] Those who harbored such ideas were most probably lower-order whites, described as "larrikins." Their behavior had less to do with possible misdemeanors by the troops and more with a sense of apprehension that wartime developments disturbed the prewar social dispensation. Hence, it was necessary to return to pre-1914 conventions, and for the socially threatened this meant that any further "worrisome" trends had to be arrested, regardless of how foul the means. Not surprisingly, for the colored troops themselves, these clashes left a sour taste. Regardless of the fact that they were fighting for the same cause as the white inhabitants, they were insulted and attacked. "The Cape Corps," it was reported, "take up the position that they are quite good enough to be used to fight, but when they come back are, as stated by one, chased like mad dogs."[49]

POSTWAR DYNAMICS
AND REMEMBRANCE

Events in Kimberley, serious as they were, did not, as far as the APO was concerned, immediately dash any hopes of beneficial postwar change. What gave rise to the APO's was that upon the return of the troops to Cape Town, General Smuts praised the troops (as well he should, one can argue, given his less than honorable role in their deployment). The APO was quick to respond that the sacrifices of the corps warranted some quid pro quo in terms of civil and economic rights.[50] The APO also embarked on a lobbying campaign, petitioning the British government and the Peace Conference in Paris not to hand over control of South West Africa to South Africa until the rights of coloreds in the area had been guaranteed. These and other pleas similar to those of the Union government were brushed aside. Gradually, the realization dawned on the members of the APO that their wartime optimism might have been misguided. Adurahman had to admit as much when he plaintively asked the delegates to the 1923 APO conference: "Can anyone mention any single advantage we gained for helping the cause of the Allies?"[51]

Although wartime participation failed to deliver what the APO hoped would be the fruits of victory, it did at a lower level and in a more generalized way open new horizons and a sharpened awareness of life beyond South Africa and the coloreds' position as British subjects. Writing on the travails of the corps, historian Bill Nasson has noted: "For virtually all of its ordinary servicemen, the war had given them a first-time experience of the empire, not only by tramping through Egypt, for instance, but by serving alongside British, Indian and other units and, in many cases, meeting men from these countries for the first time. For some, at least, the war could not help but make them more aware of an imaginative imperial citizenship as 'civilized' men."[52]

Outside the mainstream of channeled organizational politics and rarefied perceptions of empire, the wartime experience of certain members of the corps found expression in individual acts of defiance. When a former member of the corps was refused service at a whites-only café in Oudtshoorn, he responded: "What kind of place is this? I am allowed to fight for you, but I am not allowed to sit on your chairs."[53] In another countryside town, Robertson, the behavior of certain corps veterans assumed a more openly militant form. Armed with army knives they had retained after demobilization, they attacked a white man after a verbal altercation. Subsequently, it was reported they conducted a reign of fear and threatened as to "how they are going to cut up Europeans."[54]

For others, the meaning of their war experience did not necessarily translate into a heightened sense of political awareness or even aspirations, or even into open defiance. The meaning was, rather, to be found in a sense of personal growth. Sixty-two years after the war, A. Kammies from Graaff-Reinet recalled that his period of service in the corps represented a high point in his life and allowed him to look back with pride on his involvement. Regardless of the subjugation of colored people, it was not necessary for him to feel inferior. He knew his own worth and "was able to hold his head high and could look whites four square in the eyes."[55] The war experience, then, represented an achievement that could not be deleted or impinged upon by arbitrary discriminatory acts. Enhanced respect resided in the inner self, protected from the possible slings and arrows of a hostile outside world.

Particularly audible in the drum roll of Cape Corps remembrance history was the Battle of Square Hill. It was to become a synecdoche for the Cape Corps as a whole. "Talk about the Battle of Square Hill to any coloured man who knows the history of his people and chances are he will raise his shoulders an inch or two and look you proudly in the eye," the journalist and author Al J. Venter wrote in 1974.[56] While leaving room for some exaggeration, Venter's emphasis on the symbolic importance of colored participation in the war was not too far off the mark. Although Square Hill did not assume the same proportions in the national historical consciousness as white South African losses at Delville Wood or the drowning of hundreds of black noncombatants when the troopship SS *Mendi* went down off the Isle of Wight, it did maintain its vitality, even if not feted as much. In 2013 Bill Nasson could still inform a commemorative meeting at the Cape Town castle that "through these long decades" the image of the Cape Corps "still burns in our historical memory—of loyal, stocky soldiers, addicted to hobbies like darts and pigeon-racing as well as card games. Determined under fire, their bravery in the last year of the Great War was recognised by towns as well as rural 'dorps.'"[57]

Memories of the war and the bonds that had been forged during the hostilities were also expressed in postwar relationships not only between the men themselves but also between white officers and their former troops. In the countryside, former officers who had resigned from the Defence Force and entered into various business and farming ventures were known to prefer to employ Cape Corps veterans.[58] Wartime loyalty and tacit mutual understandings seemed to help bridge the gap between military service and civilian life.

For some, involvement in the Cape Corps had a further dimension in that it was on a continuum with and reinforced other forms of service and civic duties. This was particularly the case in Cape Town as far as the colored elite was concerned. A shining example was that of Cape Townian Jack Allies, a tradesman who joined the corps as a private, fought in East Africa and Palestine, and was eventually promoted to sergeant. Upon his return to the Union after the armistice, he became secretary of the Comrades of the Great War Association. He took it upon himself to look into the needs of ex-servicemen, particularly men from Namaqualand who were hesitant to return home because of a prevailing drought. Allies kept his interest in the afterlife of the corps and was responsible for its tenth memorial service, held in the City Hall in 1928. After the end of the Second World War in 1945, he was appointed national president of the South African Coloured Ex-Servicemen Legion. Allies was steeped in military matters, and his enthusiasm found a further outlet in organizing the South African Coloured Boy Scouts. He rapidly went through the ranks of this paramilitary youth organization to occupy one of the senior national positions. This kind of civic awareness in which the original involvement with the Cape Corps echoed clearly was simultaneously expressed in other areas of community life. Allies was also prominent in the Athlone and Crawford ratepayers' association; he contributed to the running of food schemes and was a keen sportsman and organizer to boot.[59]

Military service can, then, be viewed as part and parcel of a wider social mosaic. Years later it became apparent that service constituted an element of the public world through which some members of the colored elite could express themselves in terms of a general sense of civic awareness. These outlets, though they carried a certain political freight, as in the case of the Cape Corps, were not in the first instance primarily and overtly political but were seen as conduits for aspiring responsible citizens to shoulder communal duties. In this sense, then, the constitutive fibers of the Cape Corps as part of a community enterprise and commitment left a larger legacy insofar as these were transferred to and reflected in other endeavors.

Colored involvement in the First World War furthermore resonated deep into the twentieth century, as it became one of the points of reference for coloreds whenever the issue of military service surfaced. Over time it assumed a more pliable form, twisted and massaged for whatever political position was considered politically expedient at the time. During the Second World War, Smuts, in the heated political climate of the time, when the United Party narrowly won the vote for the Union to go to war, was anxious not to alienate antiwar Afrikaners, especially those whom he regarded as particularly sensitive to race issues. As a past master in political deception, he now argued, in contradistinction to his earlier justification for arming colored people in 1915, that coloreds should only be used as noncombatants, as this "has been the old traditional system in this country. You have your fighters, your combatant force, and you have all the subsidiary services done by Natives [blacks] and Coloured people and others."[60] In the event, coloreds were indeed armed and eventually deployed as subunits in larger battalions in what was euphemistically called a policy of "dilution."[61]

With the advent of the National Party in 1948 and an explicit policy of apartheid, it was not too long before the Cape Corps was disbanded in 1949. Colored people could now only be employed as laborers in the Defence Force on a loose footing and were not considered to be formally part of the force. Underlying this development was the argument that arming colored people offended Afrikaner sensibilities; that it constituted a potential threat for whites; and that in its military history, so it was claimed, Afrikaners were never dependent on the help of colored people.[62] In what amounted to a thorough cleansing of what was now considered a relic of an unwanted past, not only was the corps demilitarized, but the rupture also had to be publicly visible on a symbolic level. Colored laborers in the army were therefore issued green uniforms, as opposed to the traditional khaki; the uniform was to have no epaulets, and no military badges were allowed.[63] The outfit not only differed starkly from those worn by whites but also made it abundantly clear that colored people were not really an integral part of the new regime's army. The history of the combatants of the Cape Corps who participated in predominantly white conflicts such as the two world wars, which the new rulers in any event frowned upon as wars fought on behalf of Britain, had to be obliterated.

Despite their exclusion from the Defence Force, or perhaps because of it, the notion of a colored military tradition stayed alive. In particular, it was kept intact through organizations like the South African Coloured Ex-Servicemen Legion and annual commemorative services in honor of those who perished in the two world wars.[64] From 1951 to 1956 the legion was also involved in the futile campaign against the National Party's disenfranchisement of colored voters. In part, their war background provided the inspiration for the new battle. The secretary of the legion, S. L. Leon, viewed the campaign as a "fight against the removal of the fundamental rights that we fought for and many of our comrades gave their lives for."[65]

Over time, though, the legion opposed apartheid's institutions less actively. This was partly the result of an aging membership but also because some of the executive members gravitated toward controversial National Party institutions like the Coloured Representative Council, which was established in 1968 as a body to compensate for the loss of the colored franchise.[66] The council was regarded as collaborationist and was shunned by committed activists and also by some more moderate men and women. The extent to which the legion was involved can perhaps best be explained as a throwback to pre-1948 thinking, when a measure of cooperation between whites and coloreds, albeit tentative, existed. For the council to be considered a stepping stone for greater involvement was, however, deemed by many in a harsher new apartheid environment as inappropriate.

Notwithstanding these tensions, there still existed a strain of thought that considered the military tradition of the corps in the twentieth century, dating back to the time of the First World War, as worth reviving, even in an attenuated form. Thus N. Kearns, chairman of the league, raised the possibility in 1961 of colored people once again being inducted into the military. Initially, the government was wary, but amidst black unrest and the banning of the African National Congress and the Pan Africanist Congress, as well as the policy of gradually expanding military service for white men, it was decided to enroll colored men on a more organized basis. A unit known as the South African Coloured Corps was established in 1963.[67] Lest it be thought that this was a full revival of the Cape Corps, "Cape" was dropped from the name, and in line with apartheid thinking, "Coloured" had to be added. Moreover, the unit did not receive any weapons training; members served as clerks, quartermaster personnel, truck drivers, chefs, and waiters.

Ten years later the status of coloreds in the Defence Force changed. With the escalation of the war in what was known as South West Africa (currently Namibia), the need for more manpower meant that from 1973 colored volunteers were being trained for gradual deployment in the operational area.[68] Changing times brought about new demands. Under the National Party regime the wheel turned full circle; whereas colored troops were excluded from the Defence Force in 1949, they were once again integrated in 1973. This is indeed a history of malleable memories that, as we have seen, can be related back to the First World War.

The developments in the 1970s did not take place in an ideological vacuum. The revised role of colored soldiers had to be underpinned and justified by a different set of assumptions. On an official level the troops now had to be fulsomely recognized. P. W. Botha, minister of defense, did not hesitate to express his "pride" in 1974 in the men and was keen for "the idea to take root that the coloured population in growing numbers also regard the Defence Force as their protector."[69] In line with this kind of thinking, the military tradition of the corps was rediscovered. For P. J. Badenhorst, National Party member of Parliament and later intimately involved with what was known as colored affairs, it was an almost unbroken tradition. In Parliament he argued: "Brown people have always been willing to die for South Africa.—We think of the First World War when amongst other achievements eight coloured soldiers received decorations for bravery and in the Second World War 45,000 coloured soldiers served."[70]

The renewed recourse to tradition also called for changes in nomenclature. The name "South African Coloured Corps" was now changed back to the more traditional "Cape Corps," used in the First World War. In addition, the government sought to demonstrate its newfound goodwill in providing financial assistance for ex-servicemen to complete a memorial hall in Athlone. In 1974 the corps also received the Freedom of Cape Town Award. Moreover, further praise was heaped on the corps when State President Nico Diederichs in 1978 formally bestowed on the unit battle honors dating back to former wars.[71] On a symbolic level, continuity with the past was seen to have been reestablished. Seen in a wider perspective, the permutations of Cape Corps tradition can be linked to the conditions that renowned historian Eric Hobsbawm has identified as fertile for the emergence of invented traditions. He has identified periods of particular stress: "We should expect it [invented tradition] to occur more frequently when a rapid transformation of society weakens or destroys the social patterns for which the 'old' traditions had been designed, producing new ones to which they were not applicable, or when such old traditions and their institutional carriers and promulgators no longer prove sufficiently adaptable and flexible."[72]

Political and socioeconomic crises rapidly gained momentum in South Africa during the 1970s and 1980s. These developments called for a reformulation of the ideological basis of a state intent on staying in power, but in attempting to do so, the state was forced to make concessions without appearing weak. It was then under such turbulent conditions, which included a need for armed manpower, that Cape Corps history had to be revisited with a view, according to an army spokesman, of contributing "towards dissipating the belief that until recently the SADF has always been a most exclusive organisation reserved for white citizens."[73] The revival of the Cape Corps history, opportunistically, was also designed to serve as an agent for social cohesion within colored communities. In the process, the past was once again invoked to establish a sense of continuity, even if it could be seen as contrived. In 1972 Staff Sgt. J. Cupido, later to become an officer in the corps, drew upon the history of the corps to convince the skeptical: "The Cape Corps was the one unifying force amongst our people. It had no dividing lines, knew no political affiliation and no social difference. It was a bond binding us all together in service to our country."[74]

Although the corps had a certain pride of place in pre-1948 communities, it was somewhat ambitious, if not disingenuous, to think that the earlier reputation of the corps could simply and smoothly be transmitted to the apartheid dispensation as if nothing had happened in between. While communities generally used to revere the tradition of the old corps, they had serious reservations about the new corps.[75] The ill-fated tricameral parliamentary system of the 1980s and the rise of the United Democratic Front in opposition to that system made it increasingly difficult to project the corps as a unifying force. In the same way in which coloreds in the tricameral system were rejected as junior partners to the National Party, the corps was seen as the handymen of the Defence Force. This association was neatly encapsulated by a young person when he was interviewed in Cape Town in 1984: "I don't vote for any dummy team and I wouldn't be fighting for the whites."[76]

A U T H O R   B I O G R A P H Y

Albert Grundlingh is professor of history at Stellenbosch University, South Africa. He has published widely in the broadly defined field of social and cultural history, specializing in the history of war and society, as well as sport and society.

N O T E S

1   South African terminology calls for a brief explanation. The term "colored" refers to mixed-race people, and the term "black" refers to African people. The term "native" in South Africa, meaning "black," is old-fashioned and considered pejorative.

2   Bill Nasson, "War Opinion in South Africa, 1914," *Journal of Imperial and Commonwealth History* 23, no. 2 (1995): 256.

3   "Coloured Men and the War," *Cape Times*, September 1, 1914.

4   "Extracts from Letters Received," *APO*, September 5, 1914.

5   "The Coloured Citizens' War Relief Fund," *APO*, September 19, 1914.

6   "Liberty and Justice," *APO*, August 7, 1915. See also "Coloured People Take the Lead," *APO*, September 5, 1914.

7   "Liberty and Justice."

8   "White and Black after the War," *APO*, November 13, 1915.

9   Gavin Lewis, *Between the Wire and the Wall: A History of South African "Coloured" Politics* (Cape Town: Palgrave Macmillan, 1987), 85. See also Nasson, "War Opinion," 258.

10   Mohamed Adhikari, *Not White Enough, Not Black Enough: Racial Identity in the South African Coloured Community* (Athens: Ohio University Press, 2005), 77.

11   "The APO Volunteer Corps," *APO*, September 5, 1914.

12   "Coloured Men on the European Front," *Pretoria News*, May 14, 1917.

13   Acts of the Union of South Africa, Act 13 of 1912, 193.

14   "General Botha's Return," *APO*, July 24, 1915.

15   See Peter Warwick, *Black People and the South African War, 1899–1902* (Cambridge: Cambridge University Press, 1983), 14.

16   "Parliamentary Debates," *Cape Times*, December 7, 1915.

17   See, for example, J. de Villiers, "Die Kaapse Regiment, 1806–1817," *South African Historical Journal* 7 (1975): 10–32. A short factual review covering the whole of the nineteenth century can be found in Ivor D. Difford, *The Story of the 1st Battalion Cape Corps, 1915–1919* (Cape Town: Horters Ltd., 1920), 1–6.

18   Smuts to Merriman, October 27, 1916, in *Selections from the Smuts Papers*, vol. 3, ed. Keith Hancock and Jean van der Poel (Cambridge: Cambridge University Press, 1966). See also Smuts to Buxton, August 28, 1915, Archives of the Governor-General (GG) 545/9/93/56, Transvaal and Central Archives Depot (hereafter TCAD), National Archives Building, Pretoria, South Africa.

19   See Saul Dubow, "Race, Civilisation and Culture: The Elaboration of Segregationist Discourse in the Inter-war Years," seminar paper, African Studies Institute, University of the Witwatersrand, March 1986, 7.

20   "Battalion of Coloured Men," *Cape Times*, September 13, 1915.

21   Difford, *1st Battalion Cape Corps*, 24.

22   H. Hands to Director of War Recruitment, August 13, 1917, World War I Imperial Service Details (WWI ISD) 25/651, South African Defence Force Archives (hereafter SADFA), Pretoria, South Africa.

23   A. J. B. Desmore, *With the 2nd Cape Corps thro' Central Africa* (Cape Town: Citadel Press, 1920), 6.

24   "Duty and Honour," *APO*, September 18, 1915.

25   "The Cape Corps," *APO*, October 30, 1915.

26   Difford, *1st Battalion Cape Corps*, 23, 26.

27   Ibid., 24.

28   Desmore, *With the 2nd Cape Corps*, 7.

29   See "Coloured Recruiting," *Cape Times*, October 26, 1915; and Difford, *1st Battalion Cape Corps*, 22. This observation is also based on an interview I had with Mr. A. Kammies, a former member of the Cape Corps, at Graaff-Reinet on October 13, 1980.

30   J. W. Watson to J. X. Merriman, undated, file 620, J. X. Merriman Papers, National Library Cape Town.

31   Col. S. M. Pritchard, memorandum, undated (probably 1918), Archives of the Government Native Labour Bureau (GNLB) 187/1217/14/D 10, TCAD.

32   F. R. Cooper to Officer Commanding, August 10, 1917, World War I 1914/1918 Group (WWI 1914/1918), 1st Cape Corps, South African Defence Archives.

33   Difford, *1st Battalion Cape Corps*, 25.

34   For details, see ibid., 45–166; Desmore, *With the 2nd Cape Corps*, 30–96; *The Empire at War*, vol. 4, *Africa*, ed. Charles Lucas (London: Oxford University Press, 1924), 497–99.

35   Officer Commanding Cape Corps to Adjutant-General Pretoria, March 14, 1918, WWI 1914/1918, Cape Coloured Corps, vol. 5, South African Defence Archives; "Report on the Union Natives on Military Service in East Africa," June 27, 1917, GG 480/9/57/19, TCAD.

36   R. Meinertzhagen, *Army Diary, 1899–1926* (London: Oliver and Boyd, 1960), 200; Charles Miller, *Battle for the Bundu: The First World War in East Africa* (London: Macdonald and Jane's, 1974), 233–34; Brian Gardner, *German East: The Story of the First World War in East Africa* (London: Cassell, 1963), 144–45; W. K. Hancock, *Smuts I: The Sanguine Years, 1870–1919* (Cambridge: Cambridge University Press, 1962), 412–14.

37 APO Johannesburg to Buxton, December 6, 1916, GG 597/9/263/1, TCAD.

38 Copy in Difford, *1st Battalion Cape Corps*, 443. For Cape Corps engagements in Palestine, see Difford, *1st Battalion Cape Corps*, 167–249; Lucas, *The Empire at War*, 4:499–500; F. J. Jacobs and Jan Ploeger, "Kleurlinge in Militêre Verband," *Militaria* 4, no. 2 (1974): 42; Bill Nasson, *Springboks on the Somme: South Africa in the Great War, 1914–1918* (Johannesburg: Penguin, 2007), 158–59.

39 Interview with Mr. A. Kammies, Graaff-Reinet, October 13, 1980.

40 Brig. Gen. A. Cavendish to Buxton, August 29, 1917, GG 548/9/93/155, TCAD.

41 Magistrate Potchefstroom to Secretary of Defence, November 8, 1917, WW I 1914/1918, Cape Corps, 1, SADFA.

42 H. Bourne to Adjutant General, August 27, 1917, Archives of the Adjutant-General (AG) 42/18330, SADFA; Officer Commanding Records to Adjutant Cape Corps, December 1, 1917, Archives of the Officer Commanding Records (OC Records) 15/2/39/5.

43 Commissioner of Police Kimberley to Secretary of Police Pretoria, December 27, 1917, Archives of the South African Police (SAP) 1/250/17, TCAD. See also "The Recent Riots," *Diamond Fields Advertiser*, January 3, 1918; "Handgevechten," *De Volkstem*, December 28, 1917.

44 Officer Commanding Cape Corps to Director General War Recruitment, December 28, 1917, Archives of the Secretary for the Department of Defence (DC) 1142/1239, SADFA.

45 Lt. Col. A. J. Taylor to Director of War Recruitment, December 27, 1917, DC 1142/1239, SADFA.

46 Collyer to Minister of Defence, November 25, 1918, DC 1142/1239, SADFA.

47 Commissioner of Police Kimberley to Secretary of Police Pretoria, December 28, 1917, SAP 1/250/17, TCAD.

48 Ibid.

49 Collyer to Minister of Defence, January 1, 1918, DC 1142/1239, SADFA.

50 Lewis, *Between the Wire and the Wall*, 88.

51 Quoted in ibid., 88.

52 Nasson, *Springboks on the Somme*, 160.

53 Interview with Mr. C. van Vuuren, Oudtshoorn, March 31, 1979. Van Vuuren came to know about the incident through oral transmission.

54 Town Clerk Robertson to Staff Officer Worcester, July 5, 1919, DC 377/132/40292, SADFA.

55 Kammies interview.

56 Al J. Venter, *Coloured: Profile of Two Million South Africans* (Cape Town: Human and Rousseau, 1974), 257.

57 W. R. Nasson, "Reflections on the Battle of Square Hill, September 1918," address at Cape Corps commemorative assembly, Castle of Good Hope, September 2013.

58 Difford, *1st Battalion Cape Corps*, 27.

59 For details of Allies's career, see "Outstanding Personalities," *Sun*, October 1947.

60 *House of Assembly Debates*, May 13, 1940. See also *House of Assembly Debates*, April 15, 1940.

61 Ian Gleeson, *The Unknown Force: Black, Indian and Coloured Soldiers through Two World Wars* (Cape Town: Rivonia, 1994), 152; Neil Orpen, "S.A. Coloured and Indian Soldiers in World War II—a Comment," *South Africa International* 11, no. 3 (January 1981): 160–61.

62 Kenneth Grundy, *Soldiers without Politics: Blacks in the South African Armed Forces* (Berkeley: University of California Press, 1983), 97–100.

63 *House of Assembly Debates*, May 13, 1949.

64 Compare "They did not forget!" *Springbok*, November 1970.

65 "No Surrender of Our Rights," May 19, 1951, folder 237, box 35, S. L. Leon Papers, Documentation Centre, University of South Africa.

66 See "Proceedings of the 33rd Annual Congress of the SA Cape Corps Ex-Servicemen's Legion," December 1977, folder 237, box 35, Leon Papers.

67 Grundy, *Soldiers without Politics*, 185–86; Janet Cherry, "A Feather in the Cap? The South African Cape Corps: Ruling Class Ideology and Community Opposition," in *Reform and Response: Selected Research Papers on Aspects of Contemporary South Africa*, ed. Linda Cooper and Dave Kaplan (Cape Town: University of Cape Town, 1986), 121–22.

68 Grundy, *Soldiers without Politics*, 185–86; Cherry, "A Feather in the Cap?," 121–22.

69 *House of Assembly Debates*, September 9, 1974.

70 Ibid.

71 Grundy, *Soldiers without Politics*, 160–61; Cherry, "A Feather in the Cap?," 122; speech by Prime Minister B. J. Vorster, November 28, 1974, in *Debates of the Coloured Representative Council* (Cape Town), col. 33.

72 Eric Hobsbawm, "Introduction: Inventing Traditions," in *The Invention of Tradition*, ed. Eric Hobsbawm and Terence Ranger (Cambridge: Cambridge University Press, 1983), 4.

73 C. J. Nöthling, "Blacks, Coloureds and Indians in the SA Defence Force," *South Africa International* 11, no. 1 (July 1980): 30.

74 "Kaapse Korps Herleef," *Paratus*, August 8, 1972.

75 Grundy, *Soldiers without Politics*, 177.

76 "Objector on the Street," *Objector*, August 5, 1984.

On the Political "Warpath"
Native Americans and Australian Aborigines after the First World War

John Maynard

In the wake of the First World War, Indigenous peoples in the United States and Australia joined a global push by those on the margins for self-determination, justice, and equality. This article focuses on and discusses two organizations that formed during this turbulent global time period: the Australian Aboriginal Progressive Association (AAPA) in Australia and the Mission Indian Federation (MIF) in the United States. A comparison of the two organizations reveals the strategies they employed in their fight for land, for citizenship, for the protection of their children, and for the mobilization of non-Indigenous support. Both organizations faced powerful government opposition in both countries.

I confess that this article is not intended to be a theoretical interpretation of the two groups but is more about restoring a history that is important today for Indigenous people and communities. I derived inspiration from such missing histories of organized political resistance. Both the AAPA and MIF remain very much unknown within the historical literature. In Australia the AAPA and its impact on Aboriginal politics continue to be overlooked by many studies, and the organization remains virtually unknown outside of Australia. The MIF in the United States is similarly relatively unknown and overlooked. I intend to reveal here the impact these groups had at the time and the pan-Indigenous national agenda that both groups strongly endorsed.

In both the United States and Australia, Indigenous men returned home from the Great War with shifted perceptions of the world and

WICAZO SA REVIEW SPRING 2017

their place in it. Gaining acceptance back home within a wider community riddled with deep-seated racism, prejudice, and oppression was a devastating negative reality. Indigenous people in both countries recognized with many others globally that the war itself and its aftermath had caused a seismic shift in global and colonial power structures, and the time was ripe to raise a voice and demand social, political, and economic change.[1]

In the aftermath of the First World War, Indigenous men and women in both Australia and North America organized political platforms based on Western models but grounded in Indigenous cultural frameworks of doing business. In Australia three organizations formed during the 1920s: the Australian Aboriginal Progressive Association (AAPA) in Sydney, New South Wales (N.S.W.), in 1924; the Native Union in Perth, Western Australia, in 1926; and the Australian Aborigines Association in South Australia in 1927. The Native Union and Australian Aborigines Association both focused on local and regional issues and had relatively short terms of organized activity. The AAPA, the biggest organization of the period, instigated a national pan-Aboriginal focus, demanding "enough land for each and every Aboriginal family in the country." International events and Marcus Garvey's "Black Nationalist" political ideology greatly influenced and inspired this group. In N.S.W. the catalyst for the establishment of the AAPA in the 1920s was increased government action revoking Aboriginal landholdings and the acceleration of tearing Aboriginal children away from their families by the N.S.W. Aborigines Protection Board.[2]

In the United States literally dozens of Indian organizations sprang up in the early decades of the twentieth century, some small, some big, some short-lived, and some that battled for Indian rights for decades. Some groups largely focused on local and regional issues, while others mobilized with a national pan-Indian focus in mind. Some of the more prominent included the Navajo Chapters, the Native American Church, the Society of American Indians, the Alaska Native Brotherhood and Sisterhood, the Californian Brotherhood, the Grand Council Fire of Chicago, the Indian Defense League of America, and the Mission Indian Federation (MIF).

Of these many Indian groups I will examine here the MIF, founded in 1919 in California. This organization had a similar platform, motivations, and strategies to those of the AAPA in Australia. Like the AAPA, the MIF recognized the importance of directing its energy toward defending and mobilizing Indigenous support at the grassroots level and encouraging a united pan-Indigenous national agenda. The MIF insisted: "The control of the Indians will be in their own hands, by their electing a Captain and a council of their own people." Some of the most prominent early Indian leaders of the MIF were Adam Castillo of the Soboba Band of Luiseño Californian tribe, who served as president for most of the organization's history, and two Sherman Indian school graduates, Ben Watta and Sam Rice. The MIF's demands could not be more explicit about "the heart of the issue: Indian autonomy and civil rights."[3]

In 1920 the *Los Angeles Examiner* gave coverage to a meeting of over 150 members of the MIF who had "gathered to draw up a sort of declaration of independence." The report exclaimed in some surprise that "a former student at Carlisle (Indian School), [was] reading a speech from type written notes in English! Not Tomahawks are their weapons, but oratory. They ask [for] no scalps, but just irrigable lands." The article revealed the incredible growth of the organization in a short space of time and that the MIF clearly had a national agenda in mind: "Already more than 900 Indians have joined the federation, not to wage war but to request justice. It is hoped, they say, that shortly every Indian in the country will be enrolled in their body."[4]

The MIF recognized that malevolent forces were pitted against it, and members of the organization "were more nervous than ever about spies. Clearly they did not trust the U.S. mail and encouraged face-to-face talks rather than correspondence."[5] This fear of government surveillance and mistrust of the U.S. mail correspond to the arrest and eventual jailing of Black Nationalist Marcus Garvey in 1923 through trumped-up charges of mail fraud. Garvey, through his newspaper the *Negro World*, had delivered editorials on the shocking treatment of Aboriginal people in Australia and often cited the genocidal actions against Indians in the United States. Paul T. Hoffman, in his capacity as supervisor of the Mission Indian Agency, was certainly unnerved by the activities of the MIF: "The threat of a delegation of Indians getting together to bring before the public eye the issues of the legality and morality of federal treatment was more than Hoffman could stand. He thus began to build his case against the Association."[6] The U.S. government would contend and mount a case insinuating that fifty-seven members of the Mission Indian Federation were promoting "Bolshevistic Doctrines."[7] This was certainly an example of an early Communist scare campaign.

The MIF publicly denounced the Bureau of Indian Affairs (BIA) and demanded it abolish the allotment of Indian lands and put an end to "the Federal assimilation policy." The MIF carried the inspirational slogan "Human Rights and Home Rule" and stated that the U.S. government did "'nothing for the advancement or benefit of California Indians' and the BIA had robbed, defrauded, and denied the Indians of their land, privileges, and rights."[8]

In Australia the AAPA also had inspirational ideals and leadership. The media described AAPA president Fred Maynard in glowing terms: "As a public speaker he has few equals in the Commonwealth," and he is "an orator of outstanding ability, [who] in the not far distant future will loom large in the politics of this country."[9] Maynard, in a newspaper interview echoing the influence of Garveyism, stated that the aim of the AAPA "was the improvement of the conditions of Australian Aborigines, politically, industrially, socially and otherwise."[10] He later stated that the AAPA "consider[s] that we, as the rightful owners of this soil, have a claim upon the rights and privileges that others enjoy."[11]

In a similar fashion to the MIF in the United States, the AAPA had demanded that the N.S.W. Aborigines Protection Board be abolished and replaced by an "Aboriginal Board of Management."[12] Additionally, as early as 1924 the Aboriginal leaders demonstrated that they clearly had a national focus and agenda in mind. A letter to Marcus Garvey in New York pledged the support of ten thousand Aboriginal people in New South Wales and sixty thousand Aboriginal people nationally to Garvey and his movement in the United States.[13] It was Garvey's platform of self-determination, economic independence, cultural identity, and connection to the land that was the attraction for Aboriginal activists in Australia. Marcus Garvey proved an inspirational magnet for many international oppressed groups in the early 1920s. Bureau of Investigation records acknowledge that South Americans, Asians, and in fact people from all corners of the globe flocked to his headquarters in Harlem. One of these visitors was later famed Vietnamese leader Ho Chi Minh, at the time a merchant seaman who attended Garvey's meetings in New York.

THE AAPA AND MIF:
A MISSING HISTORY

It is only in recent decades that Indian history in the United States has to any degree focused on the early period of the twentieth century. Lakota scholar Vine Deloria Jr. had no hesitation in stating: "The period of Indian history between 1890 and 1920 remains very cloudy and unclear. Most writers about Indians seemed to think that, with the slaughter of the Big Foot band of Minneconjou Sioux at Wounded Knee in 1890, Indians became a part of America's past and they were better left there. Unfortunately, this attitude has prevailed until very recent times and has affected both Indians and non-Indians. Few people in the tribes today can give an accurate accounting of what happened to their tribes during this thirty-year period."[14]

This state of forgetfulness applied to the same time period in Australia. It was not until the 1970s and 1980s that any recognition of an early Aboriginal political movement began to trickle down to a largely academic audience. Despite the fact that I have personally been speaking and writing on the topic for over twenty years, the dearth of knowledge is still widely evident in both the black and white communities. After a recent interview on the National Indigenous Radio Service

(Brisbane) 98.9 *Let's Talk Program,* I was later contacted by Aboriginal journalist and interviewer Amy McQuire, who expressed: "I was particularly interested in 1920s activism because I know it's a gap in my knowledge, and I guess for a lot of young blackfellas as well."[15]

Histories of the MIF in the United States and the AAPA in Australia seek to address such gaps in knowledge. In exploring the historiography of the time period in greater detail, a number of important studies in Australia have examined the involvement of white people with Aboriginal people, communities, and political organizations. These studies have raised questions about Aboriginal agency within Aboriginal political mobilizations and who was really directing Indigenous movements or whether there was a genuine movement of mutual activism.[16] In this article I additionally explore the role of white supporters Elizabeth McKenzie Hatton with the AAPA and Jonathan Tibbet with the MIF and Indigenous political mobilization. What motivated these individuals and others like them? What did Indigenous people think of these white supporters? Did they see them as leaders or allies?

Both the MIF and the AAPA had sought out and enlisted white supporters to aid their political fights, as a white person could step through certain doors that were firmly locked to any Indigenous person. The AAPA found a champion in a courageous white missionary woman named Elizabeth McKenzie Hatton. The AAPA was an all-Aboriginal organization, but Hatton was afforded honorary status and given the title of organizing promoter/secretary. It was important for the fledgling organization to reach out to the people, and Hatton embarked on a statewide membership drive covering some five thousand miles to some of the more remote regions across New South Wales.[17]

In less than a year the AAPA had established thirteen branches, with four subbranches and more than six hundred members. AAPA president Fred Maynard gave Hatton a glowing endorsement: "It simply amazes me to see the interest the people are taking in this movement. I must congratulate Mrs Hatton on having organised so successfully the branches in these country towns. The difficulties of access and also opposition and intolerance on the part of the people of the provincial towns were quite enough to have disheartened any worker, but Mrs McKenzie-Hatton had gone ahead, ignoring all difficulties and had succeeded in firmly establishing the A.A.P.A."[18] As a result of her willingness to endure and confront hardship and blatant opposition, McKenzie Hatton had built up considerable trust and respect within the Aboriginal political leadership.

In a similar fashion, the MIF "membership was reserved for Indians only, [but] the Federation established the special position of Grand Counsellor for [a white man named Jonathan] Tibbet."[19] Tibbet, a legal advisor to the group, is widely recognized as playing a major role in the formation of the MIF. Tibbet was certainly an attractive option for Indian activists, as he was openly hostile and "extremely critical of the Bureau [of Indian Affairs]."[20] Looking back prior to the formation of the MIF in 1919, Adam Castillo said, "Indians had not been well organized. They had attempted to stop white encroachment and the stealing of Indian lands but had been driven away by soldiers. The Indians had appealed to the US Government, the land office, to agents and others about the loss of our lands" but were ignored. Castillo revealed that the Indians needed a new strategy with white support, and they found just the person in Tibbet: "We now know that we have heard a lot of bad reports about him from white people. But perhaps when his story is all known there will be a lot of good that can be said about him too. He is dead now. He was our friend."[21]

Jonathan Tibbet was not your normal everyday wealthy white man of the 1920s. He had grown up in close proximity to various Indian tribal villages in California and spent a lot of time with the people learning their language, culture, and history. He carried those childhood memories of kindness into his adult life, and the plight of American Indians became his lifelong concern. He settled later in Riverside, California, and made his wealth through a broker's office.[22]

Once encouraged, Tibbet took up the Indian fight with gusto. Castillo said that Tibbet "went among the tribes and personally learned of the conditions under which we lived," and he advised the Indians that the "government would listen to us when we were organized." Castillo revealed they had misguidedly "depended on the State laws to protect us in our rights to hold land, and the State has failed. We have depended on the Federal laws and they have failed." Castillo strongly emphasized the MIF position: "We believe our organization should look after the welfare of the Indians. We do not need the agents. The Federation can care for the Indians without the agents. We want to hold the reservations for all time. We believe the Indians are a nation, or a people to themselves. We need to hold land as a reservation under terms on which no white man can encroach and steal them."[23] This statement clearly defines the MIF directives as Indian driven despite Tibbet's role and support. The Indigenous organizations in both the United States and Australia were intent on being placed in charge of their own affairs.

Certainly in the case of McKenzie Hatton in Australia, gaining trust and respect among the Aboriginal communities was a slow process: "On her first approach the dark mothers regarded her with more than suspicion, believing that 'some further slimy Government trick' was being worked. They hid their babies from her, and for a very long while she could not win their confidence. The [A]boriginal mother knew that it was possible, and even probable, that her daughter would be taken away from her in early life, and virtually sold into slavery. The arrival of a police officer at the location was watched with great apprehension, and daughters were when possible, hidden away."[24] This description compares significantly to the fears and fight of the MIF in the United States. Jonathan Tibbet at the MIF conference in 1920 declared: "You all know that the agent comes on your reservation and surrounds himself with three or four policemen and then he rides up to your house and says 'here I want your little boy or little girl.' He never consults the parents whether or not he should tear that child from the house, the cry of the people who he has to protect. That system we propose to abolish first."[25] This evidence highlights that Indigenous groups in both countries held government agencies and their agents with great mistrust, especially in relation to any contact with their children.

The abuse of Indigenous children who had been separated from their families was widespread in both countries. In late 1927 the active AAPA Aboriginal community network alerted leader Fred Maynard of the plight of a fourteen-year-old Aboriginal girl who had been removed from her family and subsequently raped in her place of employment. After it was discovered that she was pregnant, the Aborigines Protection Board had her sent by train to Sydney, where she had the baby, which apparently died at birth. With absolutely no concern for this young girl's safety, the board put her back on a train to the very place of the assaults. Maynard penned a heartrending letter to the young girl, advising her that if she provided him with the details and identity of the perpetrator, he would see the man in court and made accountable for his crimes. Maynard opened his letter with comfort: "My darling little sister, I am speaking to you now as a big bro." He conveyed that his heart was "filled with regret and disgust" that the girl was "taken down by those who were supposed to be your guide through life." He continued:

> What a wicked conception, what a fallacy, under the so called pretence and administration re the Board, governmental control, etc I say deliberately, the whole damnable thing has got to stop and by God['s] help it shall.
> I may tell you and, listen, girlie, your case is one in dozens with our girls, more is the pity, God forbid, those white robbers of our women's virtues, seem to do just as they like with down right impunity and mind you, my dear girl, the law stands for it. There is no clause in our own Aboriginal Act which stands for principles for our girls, that is to say any of the white fellows can take our girls down and laugh to scorn yet? With impunity that which they have been responsible for they escape all their obligations every time.[26]

Sadly, Maynard's letter did not reach the girl. It was intercepted by the station manager, who alerted the Protection Board of its contents. The board encouraged and intensified its police harassment and intimidation of the AAPA leaders and membership.[27]

Like Aboriginal children in Australia, many Indian children in the United States were separated from their families. They were placed in the boarding school system, with many of the girls trained as domestic service workers.[28] Clearly, in both the United States and Australia, governments recognized that to break down resolve they should target Indigenous families and communal unity. The MIF leadership was also very aware that Indian girls were being deprived of their rightful earnings and that the girls were targets of large-scale abuse. A Mr. Kightlinger, who had been working in Indian affairs for over twenty years, stated: "You send your daughters down there to school and they are not properly looked after. Fifteen girls got ruined and were sent home. . . . I know just what I would do if it was my girl. . . . They are supposed to be looked after but they are not."[29] In Australia Fred Maynard recognized the end result of this government policy and insisted that the "objectionable practice of segregating the sexes as soon as they reach a certain age should be abolished for it meant rapid *extinction*."[30]

Elizabeth McKenzie Hatton's close connection with Aboriginal activists was instrumental in causing her to undergo a major shift in thinking that was decades ahead of its time. She also recognized that the diabolical system of removing Aboriginal girls from their families' care was intended to smash the Aboriginal family structure. Her political alliance with the AAPA would put her in direct opposition to all sections of the church and government and her own Christian beliefs. Hatton had no doubt of where the blame for the shocking living conditions of the Aboriginal population should be directed.[31] In a newspaper interview she unleashed upon wider society her own estimation of the Aboriginal situation:

> The position of the remnant of the original owners of this land . . . is a blot on State and Church alike. The fact that certain [A]borigines are camped under petrol tins and without certain knowledge of where their next meal is to come from is a reflection on our boastful civilization.
> We may claim that we are not responsible for the actions of the original British invaders who violated their homes, shot, poisoned, burned and mutilated the natives; but we cannot claim immunity from the conditions existing at the present time, and what should not be tolerated for one moment longer than it will take to rectify matters.[32]

Hatton, despite her place of prominence, could not be an official member of the AAPA. In correspondence she made the point quite clear that the AAPA would not allow anyone to "hold any position but Aboriginals."[33]

This was clearly of great significance to the Aboriginal leadership not just in the organizational structure but also, even more importantly, in a cultural sense. This is best exemplified by the AAPA logo: "The registered insignia shows a full-blooded [A]boriginal man with his boomerang, a kangaroo, and an emu on each side."[34]

This strong cultural identity in the Aboriginal movement was also exemplified by the MIF in the United States. The sociologist and Indian rights reformer and later commissioner for the Bureau of Indian Affairs, John Collier, observed that "intense loyalties and energies were tied up in the MIF" and that "for many or most of its members, a strong psychological, emotional, even, it might be said, a quasi-religious value" was central to the organization.[35] An observant Collier was convinced that the MIF was fighting for Indian sovereignty and that the Indian activists "resisted the work of the Indian service in the spirit of ousting a foreign power from the native soil or beating off an invasion of a foreign power."[36]

THE IMPACT OF WORLD WAR I

Indigenous contributions to the Great War and a genuine lack of acknowledgment of that contribution have long aggrieved Indigenous families and communities. Thousands of Indigenous men fought for their country in World War I, many making the ultimate sacrifice. On returning home many of the Indigenous veterans were disillusioned and frustrated that their courage and bravery were not rewarded with due recognition of their service for their country. Both the AAPA and the MIF were well informed and influenced by these issues. At the 1920 Convention of Mission Indians of Southern California, Chief Red Fox reflected that "our people have fought under the stars and stripes for American freedom, why can't we as a people enjoy all that freedom."[37]

A number of the prominent office bearers of the AAPA were returned soldiers, including Ben Rountree and Dick Johnson, who proudly wore "the returned soldiers badge."[38] Fred Maynard, in a letter to the New South Wales premier, pointed to Aboriginal courage, sacrifice, and worth during the war and stated that "when judged on the score of loyalty, fidelity, and bravery when conditions have called for the exercise of such virtues," Aboriginal men were not found wanting.[39]

GOVERNMENT REPRESSION

The experiences of serving overseas for some Indigenous men and a perceived weakening of colonial power and control played a role in encouraging the rise of organized Indigenous political protest movements. In Australia the N.S.W. Aborigines Protection Board was clearly alarmed by the unexpected arrival of a well-informed and articulate

WICAZO SA REVIEW

SPRING 2017

Aboriginal political organization fully intent on exposing the board to the scrutiny of the media.[40] The board put the new organization and its membership under constant police surveillance.[41] The chair of the board, who was also the N.S.W. police commissioner, called in a Crown solicitor to find a legal loophole that would quash the AAPA.

When this approach failed the board sought the assistance of its Aborigines Protection Board counterparts in other states in relation to Elizabeth McKenzie Hatton. The board secretary, A. C. Pettitt, requested information from Victoria regarding Hatton's activities "amongst natives in Victoria."[42] Correspondence between Pettitt and the Queensland chief protector, J. W. Bleakley, is also informative: "Mrs Hatton you refer to has been carrying on a campaign in this State for some considerable time and has had anything but a beneficial influence among the Aborigines."[43] Internal notes reveal the board's disdain for the leaders of the AAPA, "who with the exception of Mrs. Hatton are all Aborigines certain available particulars re the characters of whom are to be furnished."[44]

There is even a suggestion that Hatton herself may have been institutionalized at one point in late 1925 or early 1926: "An eccentric old white woman in New South Wales seems to have been behind this movement of fanning the agitation but has lately been removed as insane by her relatives."[45] In correspondence written in 1926, Hatton indicated that she had in fact been unwell for some time without revealing the nature of her health problems: "I am also able to report a much better condition of health though really the extensive weaknesses after these illnesses is very hard to bear."[46] Evidence suggests that the N.S.W. Aborigines Protection Board was not above insidious practices in making life as difficult as possible for anyone courageous enough to raise a voice in opposition to its policy. In 1930 the board clashed with a Mr. and Mrs. Watson, who had challenged the board on behalf of a young Aboriginal girl in their employ over access to her trust money. The board archives reveal the devious nature of the board's practices in securing "a confidential police report" on the Watsons' "business character and financial standing."[47]

The MIF in the United States, through its "consistent agitation and organization," faced similar sinister covert operations. Agency Supervisor Paul T. Hoffman conferred with the United States attorney in an attempt to prosecute Tibbet "for attempting to alienate the confidence of the Indians from the Government." By September the following year the authorities thought they had an open-and-shut case, and the "Grand Jury had handed down an indictment against Jonathan F. Tibbet, Joe Pete, F. U. S. Hughes and B. H. Jones."[48] The MIF was ready for the fight and in 1921 began publishing its own magazine, which was distributed widely and in which the MIF exposed the activities of the government. The publication targeted both the Indian and wider white community on issues affecting Indian peoples.[49] The legal battle would last for some two years, but eventually Tibbet and the Indian activists were victorious. In the spring of 1923 over seven hundred Indian delegates gathered in Riverside for the annual MIF convention. Media coverage highlighted the delight of those present, "who rallied to the cries of sovereignty and justice": "Then came the shrill whoop of an Indian and another and another. The grove was full of them. . . . Their elation sprang from the news that charges brought by a federal grand jury against Tibbet and several other Federation members had been dropped. . . . Now, federal officials had, in the words of one Riverside newspaper 'practically admitted the Red Men were guiltless.'"[50]

The MIF would continue to fight for Indian rights until the 1960s, but it was during the 1920s that the organization had its greatest victories. Only four years after the formation of the MIF, Indians were granted U.S. citizenship in 1924 with the passage of the Indian Citizenship Act.[51] Deborah Dozier writes, "They also won a critical battle in the courts for the right to school their own children in their own communities in facilities their tax dollars helped build and support."[52] Jonathan Tibbet would remain a trusted and committed supporter and friend until his death in 1930.

The AAPA in Australia did not have the longevity of the MIF and disappeared from public view in 1928, although it remained active into the 1930s. Like the MIF, in 1928 the AAPA announced that it was about to launch "an official press organ to be known as *The Corroboree*."[53] Sadly, the paper did not make it to publication, and a number of pressures contributed to the AAPA's demise, including the onset of the Great Depression, threats against the Aboriginal leadership over their children, and police threats and intimidation. In 1937 newspaper editor John J. Moloney promoted prominent members of the AAPA as important people to be interviewed by a state government inquiry on Aboriginal affairs. (Moloney was a staunch non-Indigenous ally of the early Aboriginal activists.)[54] The government ignored Moloney's advice, as none of the prominent AAPA leaders were given any opportunity to speak before the commission.

As late as 1941 Elizabeth McKenzie Hatton continued to promote her connection to the Aboriginal Progressive Society of Sydney. She wrote to the *Uplift* detailing the defense of an injured Aboriginal workman in country N.S.W.. She stated that the name of the town and the principals involved would be withheld, as no good purpose was served by providing those details. Hatton supported the case of the Aboriginal worker who had lost an eye in the workplace but did not receive any compensation or assistance following his accident. She went on to describe "the sneering we received at the hands of the four or five solicitors present before the opening of the court. . . . [S]ome of the evidence was so vile that the case was withdrawn from court and held in camera . . . and all the gruesome detail of the white man's callous treatment of the blackman etc. . . . We won the case and Fred was awarded something over £300, which is the compensation in the case of the loss of an eye."[55] Elizabeth McKenzie Hatton continued to fight for Indigenous rights until her death in 1944.

In Australia by the late 1930s, a whole swath of non-Indigenous supporters had flowed into the Indigenous political landscape. They included people like A. P. A. Burdeu, a man of strong Christian beliefs and "a white trade unionist with leftist sympathies," and Helen Baillie, a prominent supporter and feminist strongly aligned with campaigns to change Aboriginal government policy.[56] A new era of Aboriginal activists and campaigns certainly attracted a diverse and radical group of white reformers and so-called supporters. They included men such as P. R. "Inky" Stephenson, "a publisher whose strongly radical right-wing nationalism had led him into political and economic partnership with W. B. Miles, an affluent man who sympathized strongly with the social and racial policies of the German Nazi Party."[57] Both of these men tied the importance of Aboriginal connection to the continent to their own fierce sense of nationalism, and as such they lent support to the Aboriginal movement of the late 1930s.

At the same time, anthropologists like Michael Sawtell and A. P. Elkin began to take the stage as authorities on Aboriginal culture and knowledge, and they pushed for places on government bodies and committees. Many of these people, despite being well intentioned, came with their own agendas and priorities. Instead of individuals like McKenzie Hatton and Tibbet, these new so-called supporters saw themselves as the authorities on the so-called Indigenous problem. The Indigenous political groups in both the United States and Australia of the 1920s had greater autonomy and freedom to set their own political agendas and destiny than was evident during the late 1930s and onward until the 1960s. White domination of and influence over Indigenous political directives and motivations would largely run unchecked from the late 1930s to the rise in the United States of Red Power and the American Indian Movement (AIM) and the Aboriginal adoption of "Black Power" in Australia during the late 1960s.

CONCLUSION

The AAPA and the MIF provide a snapshot of the onset of organized Indigenous political activism in both the United States and Australia. Both organizations had similar platforms and demands, and they both witnessed the arrival of articulate and eloquent Indigenous political strategists with sophisticated organizational directives for self-determination. Both groups recognized the importance of attracting committed non-Indigenous supporters to meet their objectives and to overcome constructed obstacles placed before Indigenous leaders while maintaining their power and control over their own political objectives and agenda. The MIF and AAPA both recognized the need to inspire a national united pan-Indigenous movement and to confront the sinister, paranoid, and malicious government policies that were impacting Indigenous lives in both countries. Today the memory of these early political activists continues to inspire Indigenous people in their struggle for justice and equality.

AUTHOR BIOGRAPHY

John Maynard is a Worimi man from the Port Stephens region of New South Wales. He is director of the Purai Global Indigenous and Diaspora Research Studies Centre at the University of Newcastle and the chair of Aboriginal history. He has held several major positions and served on numerous prominent organizations and committees, including deputy chairperson of the Australian Institute of Aboriginal and Torres Strait Islander Studies (AIATSIS). Professor Maynard's publications have concentrated on the intersections of Aboriginal political and social history and the history of Australian race relations. He is author of several books, including *Aboriginal Stars of the Turf, Fight for Liberty and Freedom, The Aboriginal Soccer Tribe, Aborigines and the Sport of Kings, True Light and Shade: An Aboriginal Perspective of Joseph Lycett's Art,* and *Living with the Locals.*

NOTES

1 Thomas Britten, *American Indians in World War I—at Home and at War* (Albuquerque: University of New Mexico Press, 1999); Christian McMillen, *Making Indian Law: The Hualapai Land Case and the Birth of Ethnohistory* (New Haven, Conn.: Yale University Press, 2007); Timothy C. Winegard, *For King and Kanata: Canadian Indians and the First World War* (Winnipeg: University of Manitoba Press, 2012); Winegard, *Indigenous Peoples of the British Dominions and the First World War* (Cambridge: Cambridge University Press, 2011); Noah Riseman, *Defending Whose Country? Indigenous Soldiers in the Pacific War* (Lincoln: University of Nebraska Press, 2012); John Maynard, "The Politics of War and the 'Battle of Balaklava,'" *Cosmopolitan Civil Societies Journal* 6, no. 3 (2014): 83–95; Noah Riseman, "Enduring Silences, Enduring Prejudices: Australian Aboriginal Participation in the First World War," in *Endurance and the First World War: Experience and Legacies in New Zealand and Australia,* ed. David Monger, Katie Pickles, and Sarah Murray (Newcastle upon Tyne: Cambridge Scholars Publishing, 2014), 178–95.

2 See John Maynard, *Fight for Liberty and Freedom: The Origins of Australian Aboriginal Activism* (Canberra: Aboriginal Studies Press, 2007).

3 Deborah Dozier, *Standing Firm: The Mission Indian Federation Fight for Basic Human Rights* (Banning, Calif.: Ushkana Press, 2005).

4 Lee Ettelson, "Wild Dance as Big Indian Council Opens," *Los Angeles Times,* January 29, 1920.

5 Dozier, *Standing Firm,* 10.

6   Ibid., 14.

7   Mission Indian Federation, http://
    www.californiaindianeducation
    .org/native_american_history
    /mission_indian_federation.html.

8   Records Relating to the Mission
    Indian Federation Guide Sheet, 1,
    National Archives at Riverside,
    Perris, California (hereafter NAR).

9   *Voice of the North*, January 11, 1925.

10 *Grafton Daily Examiner*, Decem-
    ber 29, 1926.

11 *Northern Star*, November 22, 1927.

12 Maynard, *Fight for Liberty and
    Freedom*, 100.

13 Ibid., 32.

14 Vine Deloria Jr., *The Indian Affair*
    (New York: Friendship Press, 1974).

15 Amy McQuire, email to the au-
    thor, September 3, 2015.

16 Bain Attwood, *A Life Together a
    Life Apart: A History of Relations
    between Europeans and Aborigines*
    (Melbourne: Melbourne Univer-
    sity Press, 1994); Fiona Paisley,
    "'For a Brighter Day': Constance
    Ternent Cooke," in *Uncommon
    Ground: White Women in Aboriginal
    History*, ed. Anna Cole, Victoria
    Haskins, and Fiona Paisley (Can-
    berra: Aboriginal Studies Press,
    2005), 172–96; Victoria Haskins,
    One Bright Spot (London: Palgrave
    Macmillan, 2005); Alison Hol-
    land, "'Whatever Her Race, a
    Woman Is Not a Chattel!': Mary
    Montgomery Bennett," in Cole,
    Haskins, and Paisley, *Uncommon
    Ground*, 129–52.

17 *Wingham Chronicle and Manning River
    Observer*, August 25, 1925, 4.

18 Ibid.

19 Records Relating to the Mission
    Indian Federation Guide Sheet, 1.

20 Mission Indian Federation, http://
    www.juaneno.com/index.php
    /history/mif-articles.

21 Adam Castillo, President, LaJolla
    Reservation, "The Story of the
    Indian Federation," February 7,
    1932, 1–2, series no. 091, folder 3,
    box 16, Organizations Interested
    in Indians, Mission Indian Fed-
    eration, Riverside, California,
    1921/1927 (hereafter OII), NAR.

22 Dozier, *Standing Firm*, 28.

23 Castillo, "The Story of the Indian
    Federation," 3, 6.

24 *Newcastle Sun*, December 7, 1927, 8.

25 "Prosecution of Jonathan Tibbet
    and Others for Conspiracy in Vio-
    lating Sec. 19, Chapter 3, Criminal
    Code, 1921," 3, series no. 091,
    folder 2, box 2, OII, NAR.

26 Fred Maynard to Aboriginal
    girl, 1927, correspondence files,
    A27/915, New South Wales Pre-
    mier's Department.

27 Maynard, *Fight for Liberty and
    Freedom*.

28 Margaret Jacobs, *White Mother
    to a Dark Race: Settler Colonialism,
    Maternalism, and the Removal of
    Indigenous Children in the American
    West and Australia, 1880–1940*
    (Lincoln: University of Nebraska
    Press, 2009); Victoria Haskins,
    *Matrons and Maids: Regulating Indian
    Domestic Service in Tucson, 1914–1934*
    (Tucson: University of Arizona
    Press, 2012).

29 "Convention of Mission Indians of
    Southern California," January 27,
    1920, 32, folder 2, box 2, OII, NAR.

30 *Voice of the North*, December 10,
    1925.

31 John Maynard, "Light in the
    Darkness: Elizabeth McKenzie
    Hatton," in Cole, Haskins, and
    Paisley, *Uncommon Ground*, 4.

32 *Daylight*, October 30, 1926.

33 McKenzie Hatton to J. J. Moloney,
    1926, Society of Patriots Archives,
    Newcastle Regional Library.

34 *Newcastle Sun*, October 7, 1925, 3.

35 Mission Indian Federation, http://
www.juaneno.com/index.php
/history/mif-articles.

36 Mission Indian Federation, http://
www.californiaindianeducation
.org/native_american_history
/mission_indian_federation.html.

37 "Convention of Mission Indians,"
16.

38 *Macleay Chronicle*, August 19, 1925.

39 Fred Maynard to N.S.W. Premier
Jack Lang, 1927, correspondence
files, A27/915, New South Wales
Premier's Department.

40 Aborigines Protection Boards
were established in Australia in
the late nineteenth century to
oversee Aboriginal affairs, and,
unlike the BIA in the United
States, the boards were state run.
They would oversee every aspect
of Aboriginal life until the late
1960s (though most were recon-
stituted as Aborigines Welfare
Boards in the 1950s), controlling
what people ate, what they wore,
where they could go, and whom
they could marry.

41 New South Wales Aborigines
Protection Board, January 1,
March 6, April 24, and October 23, 1925, all in minute books,
1911–69, N.S.W. State Archives.

42 Victorian Board for Protection of
Aborigines correspondence, Janu-
ary 8, 1925, Register of Inward
Correspondences, ref. 10768 16,
Public Record Office, Victoria.

43 A. C. Pettitt to Queensland Chief
Protector J. W. Bleakley, HOM/
J598, 1926/5342, Queensland
State Archives.

44 New South Wales Aborigines
Protection Board, October 23,
1925, minute book, 1911–69.

45 John William Bleakley (Chief
Protector of Queensland Ab-
originals) to the Under Secretary
(Home Department), HOM/
J598, 1926/5342, Queensland
State Archives.

46 McKenzie Hatton to J. J. Moloney,
E 1926, Society of Patriots Archives, Newcastle Regional Library.

47 New South Wales Aborigines
Protection Board, minutes, February 20, 1930.

48 Dozier, *Standing Firm*, 13.

49 Ibid., 21.

50 Hanks, http://www.missionindian
federation.com/mifhistory.html.

51 Judith Nies, *Native American History* (New York: Ballantine Books,
1996), 328.

52 Dozier, *Standing Firm*, 24.

53 *Voice of the North*, January 10, 1928,
18; *Daylight*, February 29, 1928.

54 Correspondence Files 12/8749A,
New South Wales Premier's
Department.

55 "A New South Wales Story," *Uplift:
The Official Organ of the Aborigines
Uplift Society*, February 1941.

56 Bain Attwood, *Rights for Aborigines*
(Sydney: Allen & Unwin, 2003),
56; Heather Goodall, *Invasion to
Embassy: Land in Aboriginal Politics in
New South Wales, 1770–1972* (Syd-
ney: Allen & Unwin, 1996), 188.

57 Goodall, *Invasion to Embassy*, 236.

Veterans' Benefits and Indigenous Veterans of the Second World War in Australia, Canada, New Zealand, and the United States

R. Scott Sheffield

"One day a notice came out of the first sergeant's office with my name on it. It was my pass to go back to the states! After thirty-four months, five campaigns, and many battles, I was going home! I had made it, but my brother had not."[1] With these words, Hollis D. Stabler began his journey home and his transition from an Omaha soldier into a Native American veteran. It is difficult to imagine the immensity or complexity of the feelings that Second World War Indigenous service personnel experienced, after months or even years away in military services, in anticipating and living through their homecoming, "most filled with jubilant anticipation, some plagued by weariness, and a few haunted by the dark memories of battlefield carnage."[2] For many, the warmth of welcome, the kinship of family, and the familiarity of home deeply comforted them. "I didn't believe that I was home until I got to see my folks," one Canadian Cree veteran recalled. "I said to myself, 'I'm on home ground now. I'm safe.'"[3] Such commentaries highlight the shared humanity and commonalities in experiences between Indigenous service personnel and their non-Indigenous comrades in arms. At the most basic and personal level, the war's end was about a young man or woman returning home to families and lives left behind, each story unique though replicated countless times across Australia, Canada, New Zealand, and the United States.

Yet arriving home was only the beginning of a war veteran's experience. Subsequently, the legislative and administrative architecture prepared to aid returned service personnel transition back to civilian life figured prominently. The relative success of reestablishment measures for the bulk of American, Australian, New Zealander, and Canadian ex-service personnel has contributed hugely to the popular view of the Second World War as the "good war." The degree to which Native American, Māori, Aboriginal, and Torres Strait Islander Australian and First Nations veterans participated in this rosy postwar story is uncertain. This study addresses this gap in our understanding through a transnational examination of the administration of veterans' benefits for Indigenous military personnel in four victorious settler societies that all mobilized significant recruits from their Indigenous minority populations. The value in this approach is in helping to distinguish peculiar conditions within any individual Indigenous community or country from broader shared patterns of settler colonialism. This broader lens works dialectically with more localized studies, challenging assumptions and drawing in concepts and patterns from other experiences in comparable societies.

To date, the postwar experiences of Indigenous Second World War veterans have garnered little scholarly attention in these four settler societies.[4] Canada is a partial exception to this pattern due to a high-profile lobbying campaign over Indigenous veterans' grievances from the 1970s to the 2000s.[5] Central in transitioning to civilian life was the support available to returning servicemen and servicewomen from their governments. All four of these victorious states developed elaborate and generous packages for all veterans. Though the precise mechanics differed, each government tended to craft a similar blend of financial reward, transitional funds, training/educational provisions, employment support/advantages, access to loans for land or business development, disability pensions, and other miscellaneous measures.[6] Governments had learned from the inadequacies of programs for veterans after the First World War and sought to construct a more flexible, compassionate, and comprehensive system the second time around.[7] In each country, veterans' programs were early and massive experiments in state social welfare development.[8] The integration of Indigenous minorities into broader welfare structures was a complex process of converting Indigenous people from segregated services supposedly designed for distinct groups to inclusion in state programs designed for all citizens. The relationship between Indigenous service personnel and the benefits available to veterans was a microcosm of the broader integration of Indigenous populations into settler state welfare.

For Indigenous peoples and settler societies alike, access to military service and status as army, navy, or air force members had been an important and symbolic yardstick of inclusion throughout the Second World War. Access to benefits and quality support for Indigenous veterans, at the very intersection of their indigeneity and their "veteranness," remained a measurement of acceptance in the conflict's wake. But did one take precedence over the other for administrators managing veterans' programs? Strikingly, the patterns across the four settler states examined are remarkably similar. This transnational examination of postwar veterans' benefits for returned Indigenous service personnel reveals that the war had made a difference and that veterans' status mattered in how they were treated by the state.

However, the mechanics of administering the benefits likewise demonstrates the continuing limitations of acceptance and the circumscribed inclusion of Indigenous peoples in national social citizenship. The lingering legislative and administrative structures for Indigenous populations in Australia, Canada, New Zealand, and the United States captured to some degree the benefits and subsumed them within existing paternalistic colonial systems resistant to change. Thus, while the Second World War and resulting veterans' benefits had the possibility to provoke change in the socioeconomic position of Indigenous veterans and populations, the overall impact was muted.

In the announcements and legislation establishing programs for veterans' postwar reestablishment, the rhetoric across the four settler societies spoke strongly to the equality of access for all veterans. For example, the rehabilitation guidebook used by administrators in New Zealand contained a special note regarding Māori veterans, proclaiming that "the aim of the Rehabilitation Board has been to regard Maoris and pakehas [non-Māori New Zealanders] alike and to extend equal facilities for re-establishment."[9] A. O. Neville, deputy commissioner of Native Affairs for Western Australia, in a 1947 report from a conference on reconstruction and Aboriginal veterans, similarly wrote that the "coloured ex-serviceman has exactly the same rights under the Re-establishment Act as the white ex-serviceman and it is desired that he should be informed of this."[10] Such was also the case for Indigenous veterans in North America, where the provisions of the 1944 Serviceman's Readjustment Act (the GI Bill) and Canada's Veterans Charter were, "at least in theory . . . available equally to all returning service personnel: men and women, conscripts and volunteers, regardless of religion or race."[11] Usually Indigenous veterans could apply through normal processes and agencies, set up for returning servicemen and servicewomen. The records, both archival and oral testimonies, suggest that the rhetoric of equal access and lack of distinctions setting Indigenous veterans apart contained some genuine substance.

The relative lack of high-profile grievances in the political discourse around Indigenous veterans in New Zealand, the United States, and to a lesser extent Australia also supports the notion that many Indigenous veterans had some, perhaps sufficient, access to reestablishment programs and support.[12] This should in no way be interpreted as saying that Indigenous veterans' experiences were free of challenges or disadvantages. Rather, given the era, it suggests that a vestige of the acceptance and equality Indigenous service personnel experienced in wartime lingered after the war, at least in connection to their veteran status.

Sometimes, circumstances peculiar to Indigenous peoples required special legislation or programs, particularly in relation to the complex legal status and administration of Indigenous lands. For example, the New Zealand rehabilitation guide advised that the "need for special Maori rehabilitation measures beyond those already available within the general rehabilitation plan is, however, realised." In particular, "provision for the further development of Native lands, including tribal lands offered to the Board for Maori settlement, will have to be made" in order to "provide agricultural rehabilitation of Native ex-servicemen, within the rehabilitation framework."[13] The complexities of Māori land title and the economically nonviable blocks established through the Māori Land Court system created extensive delays for Māori ex-servicemen seeking reestablishment on the land. Even as late as 1949, 214 Māori veterans, some 4.3 percent of all Māori veterans who had been graded "A" for land settlement, were stuck in limbo awaiting farms. Understandably, "trained farmers got sick of waiting for farms and took up unskilled work, even though this sometimes cost them their 'A' grade qualification."[14]

In Canada, too, the legal standing of Indian reserve lands, which the Crown held in trust for an Indian band's collective use, complicated agricultural reestablishment. Individuals could not own a plot in fee simple on reserve, nor could banks seize lands or chattels in forfeiture of an unpaid debt from a reserve. In practice this meant that financial institutions refused credit to residents of Indian reserves. The Veterans Land Act (VLA), furthermore, required veterans to have clear title to a plot of land and be suitable for credit, which made the VLA untenable on reserves.

While veterans might opt to apply for a standard VLA settlement outside their reserve, the director of Indian Affairs acknowledged they would face serious impediments due to pervasive societal prejudice, particularly stereotypes of First Nations' improvidence: "The average Indian veteran may be confronted with a practical difficulty in seeking qualification papers from the responsible committees set up for the purpose, who may be expected to feel some diffidence about qualifying an Indian for establishment on the land on a debt basis. In other words it is feared that few Indians could qualify under the conditions set by the Act."[15] Subsequent research has confirmed that almost no First Nations veterans successfully qualified for a regular off-reserve VLA loan.[16] To make VLA support available on reserves, the Canadian government passed an amendment, inserting Section 35A, which gave First Nations veterans access to grants up to $2,320, equivalent to the grant portion of the $6,000 loan/grant under a standard VLA settlement. Though this was a much lower sum, Indian Affairs argued that the difference was balanced "by the 'more favourable conditions' that existed on reserve."[17] First Nations veterans rarely found reserve conditions favorable and struggled to translate VLA support into a successful agricultural reestablishment.

Native American veterans in the United States faced similar disadvantages accessing loan provisions under the terms of the GI Bill because reservations were likewise held in trust. Under the Dawes Act, veterans could sometimes obtain patents in fee for an allotment of reserve land, which they could then put up as security for a loan. The fact that requests for patents in fee quadrupled between 1946 and 1950 suggests that many Native American veterans sought to do so. However, they found themselves working against Indian Affairs Commissioner John Collier's Indian New Deal agenda. Under the Indian New Deal, the Bureau of Indian Affairs (BIA) had sought to end alienation of tribal lands and even to augment land in some places as part of Collier's efforts to revitalize tribal governance, economies, and cultural systems.[18]

Thus BIA officials initially resisted veterans' requests for patents, fearing they might later sell the lands and permanently reduce tribal territories. The BIA was nevertheless forced to respond, and it revised some of its internal restrictions against individuals accessing monetary value of trust lands for collateral and against creditors entering reservations to repossess stock or equipment. The BIA even redirected tribal credit funds toward individual veterans unable to access commercial credit.[19] These ad hoc measures never fully leveled the playing field for Native American veterans seeking GI loans.

Some indications of special reestablishment programs being developed for Aboriginal veterans in Australia can be gleaned in Western Australia (WA) state records, where ideas were proposed in 1947 and again in 1950.[20] However, not all administrators saw special provisions as necessary. The acting commissioner of Native Affairs in WA was skeptical about the reported numbers of Aboriginal servicemen: "I am extremely doubtful of the correctness of this figure [three hundred] and am of the opinion that no more than two hundred at the very outside were properly enlisted and attested." Because of this doubt and the fact that the "scheme which provides for white soldiers is quite capable of dealing with any native cases," the official dismissed any utility of special programs for Aboriginal ex-service personnel. He went on to say that Aboriginal soldiers were "fully informed of the benefits to which they were entitled, but very few displayed any great interest as they preferred to return to their home districts and resume the occupations they followed prior to enlistment."[21] This suggests that regular veterans' support may have been available, but it leaves unsettling questions regarding veterans' access to such programs.

However, this individual's language reveals a profoundly negative view of Aboriginal people's capabilities. He believed many Aboriginal servicemen "were discharged because of their unsuitability for the services" and went on to broaden his comments: "It is my considered opinion that the majority of the adult natives in this State are not capable of any form of advanced training. . . . I feel that these people, because of their nomadic tendencies and disregard to responsibility are not suitable for inclusion in a scheme which might envisuage [sic] their total absorption into the Community as equal citizens and a portion of the pattern of our economic life, but should be given the benefit of protection and supervision and other advantages when in indigent circumstances."[22] Views of this sort, common among Indigenous administrators in all of these settler states, bred a fatalism that undermined willingness to work or advocate on behalf of Indigenous peoples. In the wake of the Second World War, this was problematic for returning Indigenous veterans who would find such officials increasingly involved in the veterans' reestablishment.

In a striking parallel, all four countries developed separate policy structures and administrative processes to handle the cases of Indigenous veterans. The principal reason appears to be the preexisting Indigenous administrative agencies and legal architecture surrounding Indigenous populations that each state had developed through the colonizing era. Veterans' reestablishment officials often sought advice and logistical support from the Canadian Indian Affairs Branch, the U.S. Bureau of Indian Affairs, the Department of Māori Affairs, or the Australian Commonwealth and state Aboriginal agencies, or these agencies insinuated themselves and their agendas into the administration of Indigenous veterans' cases. As a result, Indigenous veterans often fell into a hazy jurisdictional overlap between Indigenous and veterans' administrations, as the following circular letter from Canada's Indian Affairs to its field staff reveals: "The Indian Affairs Branch is not responsible for veteran legislation or administration excepting administration of grants made under Section 35A of the Veterans' Land Act. The Branch, however, has everything to do with Indians."[23]

In New Zealand, Māori could opt for regular Pākehā reestablishment options or separate Māori alternatives. For those accessing the latter, Māori Affairs and the Rehabilitation Board established a joint Māori Rehabilitation Finance Committee, which "controls the Rehabilitation of Maoris," with all the powers of the Board of Native Affairs and of the Rehabilitation Board "in expending money made available by the Treasury for loans other than the expenditure on land."[24] The office manual of the Rehabilitation Department laid out the nature of the relationship:

> The Native Department acts as the agent of the Board
> in the majority of cases where rehabilitation assistance
> is afforded to Maori ex-servicemen by way of loans. . . .

[T]he Maori ex-serviceman, if fully qualified, is offered the choice of proceeding with his application for any form of rehabilitation assistance provided by the Board either through the standard procedures or through special channels in the Native Department designed to meet any peculiar need or problem . . . [particularly] in all cases where land settlement involves clarification of title and taking of title to Native land, a procedure which entails considerable specialized knowledge.[25]

This implies a smooth joint system of administration, and the government was keen to reassure veterans that no difference in services occurred regardless of which channel a Māori veteran chose. Nevertheless, differences in philosophy and belief in Māori capacity led to some disagreements in the execution of programs like trade training and employing Māori graduates to build homes for Māori.[26]

Despite claims of equality in both regular and Māori channels of re-establishment, special policies distinguished and at times disadvantaged returning Māori servicemen and servicewomen. The specific venues for Māori farm training, for instance, were on blocks or farms operated or controlled by the Native Department; *"in special cases* where no Native land is available, on the land development blocks controlled by the Lands Department"; at agricultural colleges; on Rehabilitation Board training farms; or with private farmers, under subsidy.[27] The fact that Māori access to Land Department development blocks was only "in special cases" limited Māori to the often marginal remaining Māori lands.

What is more, once they had completed agricultural training, Māori veterans were graded differently from Pākehā veterans. While the letter grades were the same, Māori veterans had an extra layer of constraining caveats:

Where a Maori was a competent farmer and capable of farming in a wide area, irrespective of whether there were other Maoris there or not, he received an "A" grade certificate for that area without any qualification. On the other hand, if it is felt that he could satisfy the same conditions only within the boundary of the Maori Land Court district in which he normally resided, his grading was limited to that district. If it was considered that a Maori applicant was up to "A" grade standard except in respect of ability to manage his finances to obtain the best results, the grading certificate indicated this by the endorsement "subject to supervision from the Department of Maori Affairs," and the department maintained supervision of the ex-serviceman's affairs after settlement until such time as the settler, in the opinion of the Maori Rehabilitation Finance Committee, was capable of assuming full control.[28]

The trouble with this structure was widespread Pākehā assumptions of Māori financial incapacity. For example, one member of the Whangerai Rehabilitation Committee "considered that ninety-seven per cent of Maori applicants for farm settlement were unable to handle their own finances, and added that after thirty-three years working among Maoris he had still to meet a Maori famer who would succeed if left to his own resources."[29] In a similar vein, Māori applicants could opt for regular rehabilitation channels, except where "the applicant was living in a Maori community or where his application involved the occupation or acquisition of Maori land or of land through Maori channels, or where the use of any other facilities provided by the Department of Maori Affairs was required."[30] These conditions would have funneled a large proportion of Māori applicants through Māori Affairs whether they wished it or not.

The separate administrative regimes for Indigenous veterans may have been as efficient as normal veterans' programs, but there are reasons to suspect otherwise. This issue has received the most attention in Canada. The onus for managing First Nations reestablishment shifted from the veterans to the local Indian agents. During Wilfred Westeste's demobilization, he recalled:

> In the final stages of our process of getting discharged and either an NCO or an officer, was talking to us, and he was giving information about all the reserve personnel, like from the University, . . . and from farmers and also some other different, like storekeepers and whatever, they wanted to put us into these groups, some joined while they were still in University, never finished University, they were to go with . . . professor so-and-so and he will brief you on getting back into University, and those of you who were in stores or whatever, and you farmers—oh by the way, he said, you Indian boys here, he says, you don't go to any of these, he said, you go back to the reserve, and the Indian Agent will look after you.[31]

This left Westeste and other First Nations veterans almost entirely dependent on their Indian agent for accurate information, for sympathetic and appropriate counseling, for completing and submitting applications, and often for a positive recommendation. Mistakes or problems in any of these categories could undermine the veteran's reestablishment.

Despite theoretical equality of access, the final report of the National Round Table on First Nations Veterans Issues in Canada suggested that in practice, "First Nations veterans faced systemic disadvantages, not faced by most other veterans, in obtaining information, counseling and applications for all of the options that were open to them."[32] More generally, Indian Affairs and the Indian Act added additional bureaucracy and regulations for First Nations veterans that resulted in delays, hardship, and frustration. Indian agents sometimes failed to inform veterans of all options, or they dissuaded veterans from options the agent felt beyond their capacity, such as education and training opportunities. The Indian Affairs Branch also used Veterans Land Act grants to subsidize their branch's overstretched welfare budget for on-reserve housing. While making houses available to veterans may have improved their quality of life in the short term, it was not the purpose of the program, which was intended to help veterans reestablish themselves in a livelihood that provided long-term stability.[33] The Canadian report claimed that "the result for many First Nations veterans was an unequal access to the Veterans Charter, and a steeper climb to successfully re-establish themselves than that faced by most Canadian veterans . . . in the crucial ten years after 1945."[34] Whether Indigenous administrative regimes were as disruptive to the reestablishment of Native American or Aboriginal ex-service personnel in the United States or in Australia is still not entirely clear, though it seems likely in light of assimilation policies.[35]

All too often, the insinuation of state Indigenous administrators into the reestablishment of veterans brought a reassertion of traditional paternalism and control. Benefits placed substantial sums of money in the hands of ex-servicemen and servicewomen, something that many settler administrators viewed as counterproductive to Indigenous people's well-being. The habits of surveillance and intervention evident in all four countries frequently led to individual veterans losing control over their own benefits, funds, and farms or businesses.

In New Zealand, one of the primary responsibilities of the Department of Māori Affairs was what the official history euphemistically termed "post-settlement supervision."[36] Veterans often resented such patronizing intervention, as evident by the following Māori veteran, who recalled that "you have to borrow money from Maori Affairs and they send a broken-down bloody Pakeha contract painter to administer your finances. You're not even allowed to write your own cheques to pay for your bills."[37] In Canada, Status Indian dependents of Indian soldiers similarly lost control over funds during the war when their Dependant's Allowance checks were sent to the Indian agents to manage for their rightful recipients.[38] This control extended into the postwar reestablishment of veterans. One veteran recalled: "I went to war to fight for freedom, but upon coming back to Canada and the Reserve, I found I was back to a lifestyle of no freedom. Once again I had to abide by the wishes of the Indian Agent and Farm Instructor. The cattle I bought with my $2320.00 was branded with the Indian Department brand I.D. [and] I could not sell one or kill one for my families [*sic*] consumption without his approval."[39] Such patronizing and overt state control seemed out of step with the freedom that these returned service personnel had been fighting to achieve during the conflict.

There are indications that even as late as 1955, paternalism permeated rehabilitation benefits for Aboriginal and Torres Strait Islander Australian ex-service personnel.[40] During a fascinating internal bureaucratic discussion in 1955 about the potential liability of the Commonwealth to pay pensions and benefits to veterans of the Torres Strait Light Infantry Battalion under the Repatriation Act and the Re-establishment and Employment Act, it was made clear that current pensions for Torres Strait Islander veterans were paid to the Queensland director of Native Affairs.[41] A report on the matter by the attorney general raised doubts about the legality of paying pensions directly to the director of Native Affairs, Queensland, but recommended a legal arrangement that would have the same result.[42] The overall pattern for returned service personnel is one of separate structures and often little direct access to their benefits or control of their own postwar reestablishment.

However problematically, those who actually received benefits were the lucky ones, as not all Indigenous service personnel even gained veterans' status and the standard array of benefits that flowed from that identity. This was particularly the case in Australia, where two groups of Indigenous people were either provided a separate, less generous reestablishment package or shut out altogether by the quasi or unofficial nature of their military service.

The first instance refers to the postwar experience of Torres Strait Islander veterans. The same rationales about Indigenous improvidence and lower cost of living that had underpinned their low wartime wages extended to veterans' benefits. A 1953 Treasury report noted that in 1944 the War Cabinet had approved a pension scheme for Torres Strait Islanders who served in the Australian Forces "based on the Repatriation Act but the rates were adjusted in accordance with the rates of pay granted to Torres Strait Islanders—roughly two-thirds of the corresponding A.M.F. rates."[43] Based on advice from the Queensland director of Native Affairs and an assessment of the cost of living in the Torres Strait, "the Cabinet fixed the pension rates at, on the average, one-third of the equivalent Repatriation pension." But rather than alter the regular benefit for Torres Strait Islanders, the Cabinet decided to shift their benefits to a different regime under the Act of Grace Schemes. The Repatriation Commission acknowledged, "These benefits were, of course, far less than those available under the Repatriation and Re-establishment and Employment Acts."[44]

Even reduced rates were denied to those Aboriginal Australians across the threatened north of the country who had served in quasi-official or ad hoc capacities and whose service was deemed insufficient to qualify them as veterans. Thus men who conducted patrols around mission airfields like Bathurst Island and Groote Eylandt, capturing the enemy and saving Allied airmen, or even those individuals enlisted in the Northern Territory Special Reconnaissance Unit in Arnhem Land were largely shut out of compensation. Noah Riseman suggests that residents in the region were frustrated and bitter at their lack of recognition and compensation when the war ended.[45] According to Yolngu wartime participant Gerry Blitner, "I didn't come out with no bars on my shoulder, no ribbons on my chest, no money in my pocket, no deserved [likely reserved] pay, no land to go back to and say this is my land."[46]

Along Canada's threatened west coast, the more than fifteen thousand unpaid volunteers of the Pacific Coast Militia Rangers, a substantial minority of whom were of Canadian Aboriginal descent, ended the war with nothing more than the right to keep their uniform and purchase their rifle for the nominal fee of five dollars.[47] The status of Indigenous members of the Alaskan Territorial Guard, formed during the Second World War, vis-à-vis postwar support appears similarly doubtful as well, though the literature is quieter on this.[48]

Given all the issues raised thus far, was it reasonable to believe that veterans' benefits could really have made a difference in the lives of Indigenous returned service personnel in Australia, Canada, New Zealand, and the United States? The mythology and popular memory that enshroud veterans' reestablishment in all four countries suggest that those benefits could and should have been a difference maker. Yet Indigenous returned service personnel were often unable to translate their benefits into a successful postwar civilian reestablishment, as was the norm among settler veterans. The addition of state Indigenous agencies into Indigenous benefits administration led to greater frustrations in qualifying or applying for programs or to interminable bureaucratic delays. Veterans who had survived the war and undergone profound personal transformation as a result of their war service grew disillusioned with the heavy-handed, paternalistic, and stifling administration of their benefits. Some Indigenous ex-service personnel gave up fighting for their full measure through exhaustion; others, despairing, turned their backs on any benefits. And, of course, some could not qualify at all.

More fundamentally, even if Indigenous veterans did have access to benefits and qualified for comparable amounts, the programs developed to smooth veterans' transition to civilian life, while quite diverse and flexible, were almost always predicated on building upon an individual's prewar foundation of work experience, education, skills, and capital/land. The marginal economic and social space occupied by Indigenous peoples in these four settler societies during the interwar years, combined with widespread Indigenous land insufficiency and generally poor access to education and health care, meant that the bulk of Aboriginal, Torres Strait Islander, Māori, First Nations, and Native American veterans lacked some or all of that foundation.

The Australian deputy director of the Re-establishment Division saw few possibilities "for normal training under the [Re-establishment and Employment Act] Scheme owing to the general lack of educational qualifications and it is felt that the practical assistance which could be rendered would be in the form of financial assistance to enable the purchase of necessary equipment such as boats, nets, etc., for fishermen, rabbit traps, means of transportation for rabbiters, etc. Any purchases of the nature indicated should be effected by the Department of Native Affairs in preference to making the money available direct to the ab-origine."[49] New Zealand administrators likewise noted the discrepancy and sought to overcome the shortfall in part through special emphasis on trade training, which Māori veterans were nearly four times more likely to choose than the national average and which Jane Thomson dubs "the one conspicuous success story in Maori rehabilitation."[50] More typically, without the prewar foundation, Indigenous veterans struggled to translate their reestablishment programs and benefits into long-term economic stability. Far from closing the gap between Indigenous veterans and their non-Indigenous comrades in arms, these provisions, so warmly remembered by the bulk of veterans in all four countries may even have widened the gap.

How, then, do we assess the intersection of indigeneity and veteran status in the years after the Second World War? The answer is that the inclusivity and acceptance embodied by military service sustained some of its inclusive magic into the postwar years. Veterans' benefits were designed to accommodate as many individual needs and aspirations as possible and in all four countries offered powerful rhetoric of equality of access. In the wake of the Second World War, such claims were not just hollow platitudes; the scale and pain of sacrifice were still too fresh and raw to permit the **rhetoric of equality being disingenuous**. Thus many Indigenous veterans were able to access some benefits and programs in most jurisdictions, giving some credence to the rhetoric of equality so hard won through military service. For some, the benefits provided life-changing opportunities; for most, the funds and programs enhanced veterans' quality of life in the wake of the conflict. However, the colonial structures of each settler state remained intact at the end of the war; indeed, these structures were reinvigorated and reasserted.

The rehabilitation of assimilationist systems was evident in the involvement of Indigenous administrations in the reestablishment procedures and special provisions developed for Indigenous veterans. More often than not, indigeneity trumped veteran status, to the detriment of returned Indigenous service personnel. The same pattern occurred writ large for Indigenous populations in the immediate postwar years.

There was some change in the realm of policy, some conditional or partial admittance to social citizenship; but on the ground, the patterns in New Zealand, the United States, Australia, and Canada were more akin to a postwar return to "normal" colonial status and social marginalization.

AUTHOR BIOGRAPHY

R. Scott Sheffield is associate professor of history at the University of the Fraser Valley in British Columbia, Canada. His publications include *The Red Man's on the Warpath: The Image of the "Indian" and the Second World War*, in addition to numerous chapters and articles. He is working on a major transnational examination of Indigenous contributions to and experiences in the Second World War in Australia, Canada, New Zealand, and the United States.

NOTES

I would like to express my appreciation for the support of the University of the Fraser Valley, as well as for a Standard Research Grant from the Social Sciences and Humanities Research Council of Canada, both of which enabled the research upon which this study is based. Indigenous peoples referred to in this study include Aboriginal Australians and Torres Strait Islanders, Native Americans, Māori, and First Nations. (Métis and Inuit, whose administrative experiences with veterans benefits were distinct, are not included.)

1   Hollis D. Stabler, *No One Ever Asked Me: The World War II Memoirs of an Omaha Soldier* (Lincoln: University of Nebraska Press, 2005), 118.

2   Kenneth William Townsend, *World War II and the American Indian* (Albuquerque: University of New Mexico Press, 2000), 215.

3   Anonymous interview, in Robert Alexander Innes, "'I'm on Home Ground Now. I'm Safe': Saskatchewan Aboriginal Veterans in the Immediate Postwar Years, 1945–46," *American Indian Quarterly* 28, nos. 3–4 (2004): 695.

4   There is some work in each country, but it is dispersed across different genres. See Noah Riseman, "The Rise of Indigenous Military History," *History Compass* 12, no. 12 (December 2014): 901–11; and P. Whitney Lackenbauer and R. Scott Sheffield, "Moving beyond Forgotten: The Historiography of Native Peoples in the World Wars," in *Aboriginal People and the Canadian Military: Historical Perspectives*, ed. Craig Mantle and Whitney Lackenbauer (Kingston: CDI Press, 2007), 209–32. Explicit examinations of Indigenous veterans are limited to Innes, "'I'm on Home Ground Now,'" 685–718; Al Carroll, *Medicine Bags & Dog Tags: American Indian Veterans from Colonial Times to the Second Iraq War* (Lincoln: University of Nebraska Press, 2008); Jane R. M. Thomson, "The Rehabilitation of Servicemen of World War II in New Zealand, 1940–1954" (Ph.D. diss., Victoria University of Wellington, 1983); and, to some extent, Noah Riseman, *Defending Whose Country? Indigenous Soldiers in the Pacific War* (Lincoln: University of Nebraska Press, 2012).

5   Indigenous veterans' organizations drove this political campaign, which revolved around claims of unequal access to benefits after

the Second World War and the Korean War. Persistent lobbying culminated in a pair of federal government reports in the mid-1990s. Subsequent reports focused on First Nations and Métis veterans, respectively, and eventually a government apology and offer of compensation to Status Indian veterans in 2003. See the Senate Standing Committee on Aboriginal Peoples, "The Aboriginal Soldier after the Wars," Senate Report (March 1995); Royal Commission on Aboriginal Peoples (RCAP), *Report of the Royal Commission on Aboriginal Peoples*, vol. 1, *Looking Forward, Looking Back* (Ottawa: Supply and Services, 1996); R. Scott Sheffield, "A Search for Equity: A Study of the Treatment Accorded to First Nations Veterans and Dependents of the Second World War and the Korean Conflict. The Final Report of the National Round Table on First Nations Veterans' Issues," Assembly of First Nations, Ottawa, May 2001; Sheffield, "Veterans' Charter Canada's and Métis Veterans of the Second World War and Korea," unpublished report, Métis National Council, 2012.

6   See, for instance, Glenn C. Altschuler and Stuart M. Blumin, *The G.I. Bill: A New Deal for Veterans* (Oxford: Oxford University Press, 2009); Peter Neary and J. L. Granatstein, eds., *The Veterans' Charter and Post–World War II Canada* (Montreal: McGill-Queen's University Press, 1998); Thomson, "Rehabilitation of Servicemen"; Stuart Macintyre, *Australia's Boldest Experiment: War and Reconstruction in the 1940s* (Sydney: NewSouth Publishing, 2015).

7   Thomson, "Rehabilitation of Servicemen," chap. 1; Jeff Keshen, "Getting It Right the Second Time Around: The Reintegration of Canadian Veterans of World War II," in Neary and Granatstein, *The Veterans' Charter*, 62–84; Altschuler and Blumin, *The G.I. Bill*, 24–33;

Clem Lloyd and Jacqui Rees, *The Last Shilling: A History of Repatriation in Australia* (Melbourne: Melbourne University Press, 1994); Jeffrey Grey, *A Military History of Australia*, 3rd ed. (Cambridge: Cambridge University Press, 2008), 198. In Australia, where pension and repatriation support had remained stronger through the interwar years than in the other countries, this motivation was somewhat less fervent. Nevertheless, through the war, the Australian government liberalized and expanded repatriation provisions. See Lloyd and Rees, *The Last Shilling*, 266, 273–75.

8   Stephen Garton suggests that the repatriation system in Australia "represented a second welfare state, running parallel to, and almost as large as, the official one." See *The Cost of War: Australians Return* (Melbourne: Oxford University Press, 1996), vii–viii.

9   *The Serviceman's Guide to Demobilization and Rehabilitation*, 23, WAII 1 DA550.1.1, Archives New Zealand, Wellington (hereafter ANZ). This pamphlet was originally intended for distribution to all returning service personnel. However, sufficient copies could not be printed in time, so it was distributed to military and governmental officials. See Brig. A. E. Conway, memorandum, February 5, 1946, WAII 1 DA550.1.1, ANZ.

10 A. O. Neville to the Minister for Native Affairs, April 18, 1947, file 135-47, State Records Office of Western Australia.

11 R. Scott Sheffield, "Canadian Aboriginal Veterans and the Veterans' Charter after the Second World War," in *Aboriginal Peoples and Military Participation: Canadian & International Perspectives*, ed. P. Whitney Lackenbauer, R. Scott Sheffield, and Craig Mantle (Kingston, Ont.: Canadian Defence Academy Press, 2007), 80.

12 For example, the National Native American Veterans Association, the only national-level association in the United States, only organized in 2004 to "represent the unique needs of Native American Veterans across America" (http://www.nnava.org/pdf/history.pdf). There is no mention of historical grievances in the stated mission or the history of the NNAVA; instead, there is a concern with the present challenges of navigating between the federal Department of Veterans Affairs and Indigenous governance structures. Similarly, the Twenty-Eighth Māori Battalion Association existed for more than sixty years before shutting down in 2012, but it does not appear to have organized any substantive campaigns regarding veterans' benefits. The secondary literature on Māori war service contains little mention of veterans' reestablishment but offers tantalizing clues about problems; see Monty Soutar, *Nga Tama Toa: C Company 28 (Maori) Battalion 1939–1945* (Auckland: David Bateman, 2008), 370–77; Wira Gardiner, *Te Mura o Te Ahi: The Story of the Maori Battalion* (Auckland: Reed, 1992), 178–88.

13 *The Serviceman's Guide*, 23.

14 Thomson, "Rehabilitation of Servicemen," 319.

15 "To All Indian Agents, Inspectors and the Indian Commissioner for BC, from R. A. Hoey," March 3, 1945, pt. 1, vol. 10712, file #43/39-6, RG 10, Libraries and Archives Canada, Ottawa (hereafter LAC).

16 During the research for the report "A Search for Equity," Veterans Affairs could find virtually no evidence of Status Indians qualifying for VLA off reserve, although the majority of identified Status Indian veterans obtained VLA support.

17 RCAP, *Report of the Royal Commission*, 1:33.

18 Lawrence C. Kelly, *John Collier and the Origins of Indian Policy Reform* (Albuquerque: University of New Mexico Press, 1982).

19 Alison R. Bernstein, *American Indians and World War II: Towards a New Era in Indian Affairs* (Norman: University of Oklahoma Press, 1991), 142–44.

20 See "Re-establishment Training Scheme for Natives," file 135-47, State Records Office of Western Australia. The file contains correspondence and reports about joint state-Commonwealth conferences on the subject of Aboriginal reestablishment in 1947 and a few memos in 1950 seeking demographic information about Aboriginal veterans.

21 Commissioner of Native Affairs to K. W. Growcott, Ministry of Post-war Reconstruction, September 1, 1947, file 135-47, State Records Office of Western Australia.

22 Ibid.

23 "Report—Welfare Division—Indian Veterans' Affairs," 1946, vol. 8927, file 68/39-1, RG 10, LAC.

24 "Office Manual—Rehabilitation Department," A/3, WAII 21 68a cn121 pt. 2, ANZ.

25 Ibid., A/10.

26 Thomson, "Rehabilitation of Servicemen," 313–14.

27 *The Serviceman's Guide*, 23–24, emphasis added.

28 "War History of Rehabilitation in NZ, 1939–65," 179, WAII 21 79a cn129, ANZ.

29 John Parkin to Director, February 14, 1944, Re 10/1, ANZ, cited in Thomson, "Rehabilitation of Servicemen," 317.

30 "War History of Rehabilitation," 177.

31 Wilfred Westeste, interview quoted in Sheffield, "A Search for Equity," 51.

32 Ibid., viii.

33 Ibid., 49.

34 Ibid., viii.

35 Russell McGregor, *Indifferent Inclusion: Aboriginal People and the Australian Nation* (Canberra: Aboriginal Studies Press, 2011); Donald L. Fixico, *Termination and Relocation: Federal Indian Policy, 1945–1960* (Albuquerque: University of New Mexico Press, 1986).

36 "War History of Rehabilitation," 177.

37 Soutar, *Nga Tama Toa*, 373.

38 Sheffield, "A Search for Equity," 21–29.

39 Howard S. Anderson, from a questionnaire filled out for the Saskatchewan Indian Veterans Association, question 16, cited in ibid., 53.

40 Such practices were pervasive in Queensland's Aboriginal administration and common across Australia. See Rosalind Kidd, *Trustees on Trial: Recovering the Stolen Wages* (Canberra: Aboriginal Studies Press, 2006); Andrew Gunstone and S. Heckenberg, *"The Government Owes a Lot of Money to Our People": A History of Indigenous Stolen Wages in Victoria* (Melbourne: Australian Scholarly Publishing, 2009).

41 G. F. Wooten, Chairman, Repatriation Commission, to the Secretary, Prime Minister's Department, July 27, 1955, A463 1956-1096, National Archives of Australia, Canberra (hereafter NAA).

42 L. D. Lyons, Attorney General's Department, memorandum to the Secretary, Repatriation Commission, May 3, 1955, A463 1956-1096, NAA.

43 Report, Assistant Secretary to the Treasurer, March 17, 1953, A1308 762-2-135, NAA. The report advocated slight increases to the Torres Strait Islander pension rates to keep them in line with incremental rises for regular veterans.

44 Wooten to the Secretary, July 27, 1955. The letter went on to say that "up to the present only a few persons have applied for benefits under the Act of Grace Schemes related to Torres Strait Islanders." Efforts to put Torres Strait Islander veterans' benefits on an equal footing were not successful until 1971, when their benefits were to be shifted to the Repatriation Act from the Native Members of the Forces Benefits Act. See R. Kelly to the Director-General, January 27, 1971, A884 A6931, NAA.

45 Riseman, *Defending Whose Country?*, 95–97.

46 Gerry Blitner, in *No Bugles, No Drums*, directed by John Burnett, 1990, cited in ibid., 96n79.

47 P. Whitney Lackenbauer, "Guerrillas in Our Midst: The Pacific Coast Militia Rangers, 1942–45," *BC Studies* 155 (Autumn 2007): 65. This reward was only for those who had served at least ninety days.

48 Charles Hendricks is silent on any veterans' compensation in "The Eskimos and the Defense of Alaska," *Pacific Historical Review* 54 (August 1985): 271–95.

49 H. T. Glover to the Director, Reestablishment Division, June 4, 1947, MP513 A1684 pt. 2, NAA.

50 Thomson, "Rehabilitation of Servicemen," quotation from 312, but discussion of this program extends to 316. Thomson suggests that much of the reason for

success in the "A" training scheme among Māori was that they were often able to train alongside fellow Māori ex-servicemen and could thus "pursue inclusion in European economic life without abandoning group solidarity or Maori social values" (315). By comparison, the "B" class trade training, via subsidized training with an employer, was under-utilized by Māori ex-servicemen because "there were few openings in Maori districts; Maoris disliked employment without their cobbers; and Pakehas preferred to employ Pakehas" (315).

Evolving Commemorations of Aboriginal and Torres Strait Islander Military Service

Noah Riseman

In 1995 Australia's Department of Veterans' Affairs sponsored a series of commemorations dubbed *Australia Remembers 1945–1995*. A review indicated that over 70 percent of Australians and 90 percent of ex-service organizations and communities participated in associated events.[1] Yet state reports suggested that one segment of the population did not significantly participate: Aboriginal and Torres Strait Islander Australians. These are Australia's two Indigenous peoples: Aboriginal people's traditional lands are on mainland Australia and Tasmania; while Torres Strait Islanders' traditional lands are the islands of the Torres Strait, separating Australia from Papua New Guinea. Historian Liz Reed argues that the underparticipation of Indigenous communities during *Australia Remembers* underscored the different agendas of non-Indigenous and Indigenous Australians. Both Prime Minister Paul Keating and Veterans' Affairs Minister Con Sciacca emphasized narratives of racial unity during the war, reflecting the Keating government's Reconciliation agenda. Although Indigenous Australians did want their war service recognized, they also wanted reparations for their war efforts and recognition of their ongoing marginalization within Australia.[2]

Flash-forward twenty years to the centenary of the First World War, and Aboriginal and Torres Strait Islander inclusion in commemorative events was quite conspicuous. Indeed, in the new millennium there has been a "boom" in commemorations of Indigenous military

WICAZO SA REVIEW SPRING 2017

service. To an extent this is a symptom of the global "memory boom," but it is also a significant consequence of the Reconciliation movement and the History Wars.[3] The Reconciliation movement of the 1990s sought to unite Indigenous and non-Indigenous Australians through new understandings of shared histories, including discussions about violent colonial dispossession. While many Australians embraced the Reconciliation movement, among other sectors of the population there was a backlash against supposed special treatment accorded to Indigenous Australians.[4]

Part of this backlash manifested as the History Wars, which coincided with the 1996–2007 government of John Howard. Conservative pundits argued that academic historians exaggerated frontier violence and child removal, painting a wholly negative, "black armband" vision of Australian history. Most academic historians and public intellectuals retorted that conservatives were whitewashing Australian history to suit nationalist agendas.[5] Indigenous military service comfortably transcended the History Wars while also supporting Reconciliation by showing a history of Indigenous and non-Indigenous Australians working together. Invoking the language of shared sacrifice and Indigenous inclusion within Australia's Anzac mythology spoke a language palatable to conservative Australian values. Amidst this wider sociopolitical context, new Indigenous ex-service organizations emerged and received support from local, state, and federal governments for memorials, marches, and services.

The boom in Indigenous military commemorations also parallels a widespread valuing of military achievement in Australian society. Marilyn Lake and Henry Reynolds, among other historians, have criticized this "militarization of Australian history." They argue that the valorization of military achievement in Australia is a deliberately manipulated act of conservative propaganda seeking to undermine public memory of colonization and to marginalize the place of Aboriginal victims of frontier violence in Australian history.[6]

Yet Aboriginal and Torres Strait Islander peoples have also demonstrated a wish to honor their servicemen and servicewomen and have been doing so since the First World War. Such practices have incorporated Indigenous traditions while concurrently asserting military service as a legitimizing claim to Australian citizenship rights. The escalation of such commemorations in recent years and its increasing recognition by non-Indigenous Australians is in keeping with the global memory boom. While it may be argued that this offers a version of Indigenous Australian history that is "safe" for conservative, nationalistic, military-focused consumption, the boom has not diverted attention from the settler violence and Indigenous resistance to colonialism, sometimes dubbed the frontier wars.[7] On the contrary, it has drawn attention to that missing chapter in the national military story. This article will chronologically outline the history of commemorations of Australian Indigenous military service from the early, locally organized events to the recent boom in state and national commemorations. It relies on a mixture of Indigenous and newspaper sources, and the newspaper sources are especially interesting because they reveal examples of Indigenous participation in commemorations that challenge some of the popular memory of their exclusion. By contextualizing this boom in the wider public discourse about Aboriginal and Torres Strait Islander history and colonialism, this article will demonstrate the ways that Indigenous and non-Indigenous agendas have shaped memorializations of Indigenous military service.

EARLY COMMEMORATIONS OF AUSTRALIAN INDIGENOUS SERVICE

Australian Indigenous people have participated in all of Australia's major overseas conflicts of the twentieth century: the Boer War, First World War, Second World War, Malayan Emergency, Korean War, Vietnam War, Gulf War, and peacekeeping missions around the globe. Common commemorative practices emerged in Australia during and after the First World War and have been adapted over the century to include men and women who served in all subsequent conflicts. Aboriginal people were sometimes included in memorialization practices during the interwar period. Local war memorials usually included Aboriginal names.[8] In 1931 the New South Wales (NSW) Returned Sailors and Soldiers Imperial League of Australia (currently known as Returned and Services League, or RSL) magazine *Reveille* launched an investigation whose intent was to record the names of all Aboriginal men who served in the First World War. The editors sent circulars to Aboriginal protectors—the administrators authorized by state governments to control all aspects of Aboriginal people's livelihoods—and published the names from NSW, Victoria, and Queensland.[9] There is also evidence of Aboriginal men being excluded from services, denied entry to RSLs, or relegated to the back of Anzac Day marches.[10]

Meanwhile, Aboriginal communities were developing their own local memorials and commemorative practices. Several Aboriginal reserves constructed honor boards.[11] In 1925 residents of Raukkan Mission in South Australia raised funds to construct a four-pane stained-glass window in the church bearing the names of the fallen.[12] Aboriginal people sometimes incorporated their own customs into commemorations, such as a "special dance of remembrance" performed by "warriors" on Palm Island, Queensland, in 1936.[13] In townships with mainly Aboriginal populations, the lines between local and Indigenous war memorial were sometimes blurry. For instance, Tasmania's minister for lands and works unveiled the Cape Barren Island War Memorial

Figure 1. Dedication of the war memorial on Cape Barren Island, Tasmania, 1937. Courtesy Tasmanian Archive & Heritage Office, item PH30/1/6674.

in September 1937.[14] Cape Barren Island's population was (and still is) predominantly Aboriginal, and photos of its dedication clearly show Aboriginal men front and center (see Figure 1).[15]

In the immediate period after the Second World War, Aboriginal and Torres Strait Islander ex-service personnel continued to participate in commemorative events on Anzac Days. Ngarrindjeri man

A salute for their war record

The Lieut.-Governor, Sir Kenneth Street, salutes one of the Aboriginal ex-servicemen during his inspection at the War Memorial yesterday. **ABORIGINAL WAR HEROISM PRAISED**

Figure 2. NAIDOC event at Sydney's Anzac Memorial in Hyde Park as reported in the *Sydney Morning Herald*, July 12, 1959. Courtesy Fairfax Syndication.

Gordon Rigney from Raukkan Mission in South Australia annually laid a wreath made out of swan feathers at Adelaide's Anzac Day dawn service.[16] High-profile Gunditjmara veteran Reg Saunders, who served in both the Second World War and Korea, led numerous Anzac Day marches; and Korean War veteran Stephen Dodd led Adelaide's Anzac Day marches for several years. In the small north Queensland town of Kuranda, members of the nearby Mona Mona Mission band accompanied the 1952 Anzac Day service.[17] In July 1969 there was even a NAIDOC (National Aboriginal and Islander Day Observance Committee) event at Sydney's Anzac Memorial in Hyde Park to recognize Aboriginal Second World War service. Pastor Frank Roberts declared to the at least thirty Aboriginal ex-servicemen and servicewomen in attendance: "There can be no greater demonstration than your presence here today of the part Aboriginal Servicemen played when the call came to take up arms" (see Figure 2).[18] In remote northern Australian communities, for decades dances and songs in traditional languages have memorialized their unique Second World War experiences.[19]

This long history of Indigenous military service and participation in Anzac Day and other memorial traditions demonstrated, among other points, an affirmation of Aboriginal and Torres Strait Islander citizenship in Australia. As Bart Ziino argues, public expressions of bereavement constituted acts of citizenship that "mediated their members' relationships to a developing national culture, as they strove to assert their values in common with those that the war had fostered nationally."[20] While Aboriginal and Torres Strait Islander people used the language of Anzac to legitimize calls for citizenship rights, paradoxically their military service disappeared from Australia's popular memory. The strength of the white digger mythology left little room for those who did not fit the imagery of what Graham Seal describes as "the stereotypical representation of the ideal Australian as a tall, tough, laconic, hard-drinking, hard-swearing, hard-gambling, independent, resourceful, anti-authoritarian, manual labouring, itinerant, white male."[21] Gradually a dominant narrative emerged within Indigenous communities that Anzac Days and other commemorative practices wholly excluded them.

REVIVING INDIGENOUS PRACTICES

Historian Jay Winter argues that the 1970s marked the global rise of so-called hyphen groups such as Jewish Americans and African Americans asserting themselves in national war narratives. In Australia the emergence of "hyphen" interests grew primarily out of two postwar phenomena. First, as Bruce Scates notes, from the late 1950s new emigrants from southern and eastern Europe demanded to use memorials for their own commemorative practices. The other factor was hitherto marginalized groups' assertive demands to participate in Anzac Day services. Joy Damousi argues that fighting for recognition represented affirmation of a group's sacrifice and memory.[22] Aboriginal and Torres Strait Islander families were not immune to these processes, particularly in the wake of the struggles for civil rights and self-determination in the 1960s and 1970s. By the 1980s Indigenous people, too, were demanding the affirmation of servicemen and servicewomen's "hyphen" identities as Indigenous *and* Australian.

In 1985 a group of Aboriginal veterans formed the National Aborigines and Islander Ex-Services Association and petitioned to march in Melbourne's Anzac Day parade. This would have broken with tradition, for at that time rules required ex-service personnel to march with their units. Victorian RSL President Bruce Ruxton denied their request, arguing that marching as their own group would make the gap "wider and wider between black and white."[23] Ruxton embodied what cultural studies scholar Fiona Nicoll refers to as a "conservative digger-nationalist" ideology, positing the notion of a single "digger" identity—digger being a colloquial term for Australian soldiers. This contrasted with the "hyphen" idea that "diggers" could accommodate diversity and difference.[24] Aboriginal Vietnam veteran Darryl Wallace expressed why they wanted to march as their own contingent: "It is very important that people . . . see that black fellows had the courage and the guts to lay down their lives for this country. If they don't see black fellows marching as a group, they'll never know that."[25] Wallace's statement aligns with Damousi's observation that "to lose the recognition of their specific contribution from public commemoration would mean they would endure another loss: that of relinquishing *their* special place in the memory of war."[26]

Ultimately Ruxton's prediction of division came true: once excluded from Melbourne's main Anzac Day march, the National Aborigines and Islander Ex-Services Association organized its own march through the suburb of Northcote. Where the idea of unity and division sits here is complex, because the Aboriginal veterans wanted to participate in the main Anzac Day ceremonies to affirm their identities as both Aboriginal and Australian. Ruxton refused to recognize this dual identity, instead suggesting that the veterans had to choose to be either Aboriginal or Australian.

Sources conflict about what year(s) the Anzac Day march in Northcote went ahead between 1985 and 1988. Aboriginal Vietnam veteran Darryl Wallace recalls that there were about thirty marchers, about half of them Koories and the other half non-Indigenous allies.[27] In 1987 the National Aborigines and Islander Ex-Services Association applied for a grant from the Bicentennial Authority to erect a memorial to Aboriginal and Torres Strait Islander people killed in Australia's wars. After the authority rejected the application, Aboriginal veterans Stewart Murray and Darryl Wallace constructed a simple memorial: a base of rocks topped with a cross, erected in front of the Aborigines Advancement League. The cross had the names of Australia's overseas wars and the words "Lest we forget, RIP."[28] The National Aborigines and Islander Ex-Services Association disbanded when convener Murray died and Wallace became ill.[29]

Notwithstanding opposition from the RSL, other non-Indigenous Australians supported this and similar initiatives to recognize Aboriginal and Torres Strait Islander military service. After reading an article about Ruxton's rejection of the National Aborigines and Islander Ex-Services Association, in 1988 private citizen Honor Thwaites erected a small memorial to Aboriginal and Torres Strait Islander military service on Mount Ainslie behind the Australian War Memorial (AWM) in Canberra. The simple plaque on a stone reads: "Remembering the Aboriginal people who served in the Australian Armed Services."[30] In 1991 the Kombumerri Aboriginal group from the Gold Coast dedicated a memorial entitled *Yugambeh*. The memorial contains a plaque inscribed, "We honour those who served in the armed forces and those who made the supreme sacrifice. The symbolism of this rock serves to highlight the role played by indigenous Australians in defence of this country."[31]

WICAZO SA REVIEW

SPRING 2017

The emergence of the Reconciliation movement reset the agenda for commemorations of Indigenous military service. In 1991 the Australian government set up the Council for Reconciliation, and the importance of recognizing Australia's shared histories was firmly on the national agenda. In his landmark 1992 Redfern Park address, Prime Minister Keating declared: "Imagine if non-Aboriginal Australians had served their country in peace and war and were then ignored in history books."[32] Amidst this climate, in 1993 Aboriginal Korean War veteran Cec Fisher led a delegation with the Kombumerri group and petitioned the South Queensland RSL for permission to lead the Gold Coast Anzac Day march. Unlike in Melbourne eight years earlier, the Gold Coast RSL voted in favor of the initiative. A contingent of about fifty personnel and their families led the march with an Aboriginal-designed banner. The three lead marchers carried Australian, Aboriginal, and Torres Strait Islander flags, affirming the marchers' multiple identities. The Gold Coast initiative did not receive significant press,[33] yet it marked a significant turning point: Indigenous groups were still initiating commemorations, and during the Reconciliation movement of the early 1990s, non-Indigenous organizations were receptive.

THE HISTORY WARS INTERVENE

Though the Reconciliation movement continued in the late 1990s, the 1996 election of the conservative Howard government politicized Indigenous history. These so-called History Wars would also have the ironic effect of increasing the visibility of Indigenous military service.

The turning point was in November 1998, when the governor-general, Sir William Deane, inadvertently sparked a controversy. While launching historian Ken Inglis's book *Sacred Places*, Deane stated, "There are few memorials to the colonial conflicts of the 19th century—certainly almost none, at least of an official kind, to the Aborigines who were slaughtered in the 'Black Wars' of that period."[34] Inglis's own speech called for the AWM to incorporate the frontier wars, arguing, "Here, as we approach the centenary of federation, is a challenge and an opportunity for the Australian War Memorial to make a distinctive contribution to the task of reconciliation." Several media outlets wrongly attributed Inglis's quote to Deane, and debates over the frontier wars' inclusion in the AWM waged for weeks.[35] This was neither the first nor the last time that this question arose,[36] but it was the most extensive. Early on, the AWM declared its position that "this and other pre-Federation and colonial issues properly come within the responsibility of the National Museum of Australia."[37] RSL representatives condemned the proposition, instead suggesting a new memorial to frontier conflicts.[38]

Though several arguments rested on the legalities of whether frontier violence constituted a war, the debates also exposed underlying disquiets about the colonization of Australia. Several scholars have written about how white anxieties over Australia's violent settlement play out through veneration of the Anzac legend, succinctly described by historians Marilyn Lake and Henry Reynolds as, "In proving their manhood—brave, firm, loyal and steadfast—these men [First World War servicemen] (so it was said) had proven our nationhood."[39] Clemence Due asserts that "commemorations of war and the Anzacs are considered celebrations of what it means to be Australian, and . . . such constructions deny the experiences of Indigenous Australians in *their* wars to defend their country from colonization."[40] Nicoll further argues that "the exclusion of frontier wars from official military commemoration is a powerful symbolic means by which white Australian subjectivity is affirmed and Indigenous Australians are kept in their place as controllable objects of domestic policy."[41] Damousi concludes that, since the very legitimacy of Australia is premised on the dispossession of Indigenous people, their loss and grief inevitably cannot form part of the nation's military mythology.[42]

Prime Minister Howard did not accept the arguments to incorporate frontier wars in the AWM, instead reasoning, "But my understanding of the High Court in the Mabo decision (is that it) did not regard the British as having conquered the then Australian land mass, but rather settled it, and therefore, if you want to be legalistic about it, the state of war didn't exist."[43] Howard's logic evinces Due's argument: "Once the wars fought by Indigenous Australians are no longer open for consideration at the same level as those fought by post-colonial Australia, the path is open for non-Indigenous histories to take centre stage and create and legitimate a white Australia."[44]

Questions about including the frontier wars in Australia's military canon added fuel to the History Wars. In contrast, commemorating Aboriginal and Torres Strait Islander service in Australia's overseas conflicts seemed a safe approach that did not challenge national mythologies or threaten white Australians' comfort. In 1999 during NAIDOC week, there was a service at Canberra's Aboriginal Memorial. Glenda Humes, daughter of Reg Saunders, addressed the crowd and spoke of the motivations and hardships experienced by her father, uncle, and other Indigenous servicemen and servicewomen. She remarked, "I think it was more to do with this was their country and they wanted to defend it." Humes also stated, "It was quite an achievement, given that at the time he [Uncle Harry] did that, Aboriginal people didn't even have citizenship rights."[45] Humes's remarks presented a history of past Indigenous exclusion while concurrently affirming their commitment to Australia; indeed, she affirms Indigenous defense of Australia since time immemorial.

This narrative fit a Reconciliation framework while also transcending the History Wars through the message of "unity" as Australians. It was a "safe" narrative that did not challenge the Anzac legend but rather called for the Anzac legend to include Indigenous Australians. Alistair Thomson argues that "the stories and the meanings that do not fit today's public [Anzac] narrative are still silenced or marginalised, and at best only resurface within a sympathetic particular public."[46] Through the language of Reconciliation, Indigenous Australians found the means to reach a sympathetic public, a sharp change from the supposed divisiveness inferred by Bruce Ruxton in the 1980s.

THE BOOM IN INDIGENOUS COMMEMORATION

In late 2000 the newly formed Aboriginal and Torres Strait Islander Veterans and Services Association approached the Perth RSL to march as a group in Perth's 2001 Anzac Day march. The RSL not only granted permission but invited the group to lead the march. At least sixty Aboriginal and Torres Strait Islander men and women marched, receiving some of the loudest cheers. Organizer Phil Prosser said, "It is quite important for the indigenous people of Australia to be able to go public and show that we did actually represent our people and the whole of Australia."[47] The Perth march continued the long tradition of Indigenous-organized commemorations, but now there were more media attention and institutional support.

More Aboriginal and Torres Strait Islander ex-service organizations emerged in the 2000s. One of the more successful groups, founded in 2005, was Perth-based Honouring Indigenous War Graves (HIWG). Aboriginal Vietnam veteran John Schnaars founded the organization to dedicate remembrance plaques at the gravesites of deceased Aboriginal servicemen and servicewomen. The plaques are actually entitlements for any service personnel deemed eligible by the Australian War Graves Commission. For Aboriginal families, the HIWG headstone ceremonies represent not only tribute to the servicemen's sacrifices but also acknowledgment that they had *not* been recognized for decades. Since 2005 HIWG has performed over 180 ceremonies across Western Australia, doing between fourteen and eighteen per year, and it marches as a group on Anzac Day in Perth. Funding for HIWG comes from a mix of fund-raising, sponsorship from local RSLs, the Western Australian Department of Aboriginal Affairs, and other corporate donations. HIWG raised funds to construct memorials in Broome to the Second World War Coastwatcher Z Special Unit and in Bruce Rock to honor Papua New Guineans.[48] The public and private sectors' willingness to support HIWG attests to the appeal of HIWG's reconciliation message.

In 2007 the Babana Men's Group planned the first Coloured Diggers march through Sydney's heavily Aboriginal neighborhood of Redfern. This march attracted seventeen veterans and about five hundred family members, friends, and other supporters. Though not condemning the march per se, NSW RSL President Bill Crews expressed disappointment, because "it's unfortunate they don't feel they will get the attention they need at those [regular] services." The march organizer, Pastor Ray Minniecon (whose two brothers served in Vietnam), responded that holding a separate Aboriginal Anzac Day march was not meant to be divisive. Minniecon said that it was an opportunity to encourage participation, since "a lot of our people don't march on Anzac Day and we're simply trying to give them the opportunity to be recognised and acknowledged in the same way that anyone who served their country should be recognised." Marchers, particularly veterans, commented about how it was an emotional event that filled them with pride. Many had previously marched on Anzac Days, while others had previously spurned Anzac Day marches because of histories of their ancestors being excluded from the normal parades. The NSW RSL subsequently clarified its position to be in support of the Redfern march.[49] The Coloured Diggers march was so successful that it has since become an annual event and grown in scope. Each year the Coloured Diggers march has a different thematic focus, such as the contributions of Indigenous servicewomen or prisoners of war. The message of reconciliation permeates the Coloured Diggers marches, with Pastor Minniecon's prayer at the first march saying, "May we as a nation come to fully acknowledge the contribution that the Aboriginals and Torres Strait Islanders have made to the defence of our land."[50]

The other focal point for commemorations of Indigenous military service is now Reconciliation Week around May 26. In 2006 Aunty Dot Peters, a Wurundjeri Elder from Healesville near Melbourne, organized a ceremony at Melbourne's Shrine of Remembrance with the support of the Victorian RSL to honor Aboriginal and Torres Strait Islander military service. Aunty Dot then wrote to the minister for veterans' affairs, and since 2007 the Department of Veterans' Affairs has sponsored services during Reconciliation Week in six capital cities.[51] Just the timing of these services—during Reconciliation Week—highlights the key theme of the ceremonies. They regularly include politicians and current and former Indigenous service personnel, and the local Indigenous organizers cater the events to the interests of their communities.[52]

The Reconciliation services also served as a springboard to pursue more permanent memorials to Indigenous service. Since the late 1990s there have been several small Aboriginal and Torres Strait Islander military service memorials erected across the country at places including Yirrkala, Northern Territory (1995); Launceston, Tasmania (1999);

Thursday Island, Queensland (2001); Point Pearce, South Australia (1999); Collie, Western Australia (2000); Fremantle, Western Australia (2001); Warrnambool, Victoria (2010); and the Tiwi Islands, Northern Territory (2016).[53] In 2000 the Department of Veterans' Affairs office building in Canberra was named Lovett Tower in honor of the Gunditjmara family from Western Victoria whose family has served in all Australian conflicts since the First World War. The AWM has unofficially adopted and appropriated the Mount Ainslie memorial and since 2004 has hosted an Aboriginal Anzac Day service there led by the Aboriginal and Torres Strait Islander Veterans and Services Association.[54]

Pushes for larger memorials began in Adelaide and Sydney in earnest in 2008. Both campaigns were long and required Aboriginal organizations to build alliances with local and state governments, RSLs, and the private sector. The Adelaide group formed the Aboriginal and Torres Strait Islander War Memorial Committee and launched a fund-raising appeal. They documented the history of South Australian Aboriginal communities' military service and even produced a short documentary. The glossy appeal brochure indicated that they were "seeking support from individuals, corporations and groups who recognise the importance of expressing gratitude for the efforts made by our first Australians in the defence of Australia."[55] Eventually the South Australian appeal raised $1 million. The memorial design consciously blends traditional Indigenous art with common European memorial tropes, such as a wall, people's names, and statues. The two statues depict an Aboriginal serviceman and servicewoman, thus being consciously gender inclusive (see Figures 3 and 4). The common trope of remembering the forgotten was front and center at the memorial's November 2013 dedication. The deputy chair of the Aboriginal and Torres Strait Islander War Memorial Committee, Ngarrindjeri ex-serviceman Frank Lampard, declared to resounding applause, "Eventually time renders any link too remote, and unrecorded sacrifice is forgotten. . . . Well I'm proud to say that lack of recognition ends today!"[56] In Brisbane a similar Aboriginal and Torres Strait Islander Dedicated Memorial Committee has been raising funds for a new memorial in ANZAC Square to be completed in 2018.[57]

The City of Sydney commissioned an artwork in Hyde Park to commemorate Indigenous defense contributions entitled *Yininmadyemi— Thou didst let fall*, which was completed in March 2015. The sculpture is quite different from traditional war memorials in that it is four standing bullets and three fallen shells. Passersby do not see that the memorial is about Indigenous Australians until they approach the artwork and read the accompanying plaques (see Figure 5). The text mentions that Aboriginal and Torres Strait Islander people have served in all conflicts yet returned home to continuing inequalities.[58]

Figure 3. Adelaide's Aboriginal and Torres Strait Islander War Memorial after the dedication ceremony, November 2013. Photograph by the author.

Figure 4. Plaque at the entrance to Adelaide's Aboriginal and Torres Strait Islander War Memorial. Photograph by the author.

Winter notes that "all war memorials have a 'shelf-life,' a bounded period of time in which their meaning relates to the concerns of a particular group of people who created them or use or appropriate them as ceremonial or reflective sites of memory. That set of meanings is never

Figure 5. Sydney's sculpture *Yininmadyemi—Thou didst let fall*. Photograph by the author.

permanent."[59] One way changing meanings are already emerging is through the lingering question of commemorating the frontier wars.

RETURNING TO THE FRONTIER

Prominent Australian historian and public intellectual Henry Reynolds is critical of the boom in Indigenous military service commemorations. Though he does not disparage the contributions of Aboriginal and Torres Strait Islander servicemen and servicewomen, he critiques commemorative activities on two grounds. First, they are part of a larger trend of the militarization of Australian history. Second, they "draw attention away from the armed conflict that was the central feature of the relationship between settlers and the Indigenous nations."[60] Reynolds's assertion implies a false either/or dichotomy: either we commemorate Aboriginal and Torres Strait Islander military service since the Boer War *or* we commemorate the frontier wars.

In fact, the recent boom has opened a new, post–History Wars space for the questions of if and how to include the frontier wars in Australia's military history. Media reports about Indigenous military commemorations regularly ask the next logical question: What about the frontier wars?[61] Indigenous commemorations have begun referencing the frontier wars. During their 2007 NAIDOC Week speeches at Canberra's Aboriginal War Memorial, Aboriginal former officers Margo Weir and Tom Slockee described the memorial as a place to commemorate Indigenous warriors, both those who served with the Australian

military *and* those who fought to resist colonization. The theme of Redfern's 2015 Coloured Diggers march was "To Our Warrior Forebears"; the event invitation began, "To our warrior forebears who fought for their traditional lands here in Australia. . . . [W]e are merely part of a continuous warrior tradition."[62] Even the text accompanying Sydney's Hyde Park sculpture alludes to the frontier wars, opening with the words, "Aboriginal and Torres Strait Islander people have always defended their country."[63] Liza-Marie Syron describes *Yininmadyemi* as "a monument that aims to disorientate visitors temporarily, challenging not only the social, cultural, and political narratives of Australians at war but also those that surround pre-colonial history and the memory of Aboriginal existence. *Yininmadyemi* is anti-memorial: it unsettles."[64]

An earlier, distinct example is an obelisk erected in Mount Isa, Queensland, in 1984 to commemorate the Battle Mountain massacre of the Kalkadoon people. Elizabeth Furniss describes this memorial as an example of the "Anzac-isation" of frontier resistance to colonialism. She argues, "The Anzac myth, like the narratives of discoverers, firsts, and pioneers, has both a conservative and creative dimension, and can be metaphorically extended in some quite surprising and innovative ways to incorporate new events and figures within mythic traditions of Australia's past."[65]

A more dramatic example of the "Anzac-isation" of the frontier wars occurred in 2011 when members of the Aboriginal Tent Embassy tacked themselves onto the end of Canberra's Anzac Day march. They carried a banner that read "Lest We Forget the Frontier Wars," and their lead marcher, Mick Thorpe, carried a boomerang and a nulla nulla (hunting stick) and wore the medals of his grandfather who died on the Somme in 1918. Nicoll argues that Thorpe embodied a dual commemoration, inscribing the Anzac legend (or "Anzac-ising") on the frontier wars. Marchers also carried signs with the names of sites of Indigenous resistance and/or massacres, mimicking the non-Indigenous tradition of inscribing the names of overseas battles on war memorials.[66]

Police initially tried to block the marchers, but then participants convinced the police that they were *participants* in the Anzac Day march, not protesters. Aboriginal marcher Michael Anderson recalls, "It was very emotional when we went through and . . . the people applauded us. That was quite a shock to a lot of us. . . . Black people were crying who were carrying those placards because . . . we weren't sure what sort of reception we were going to get up there and whether people thought it was a protest and it was an inappropriate time to protest. But like I told the police at the beginning, this is not a protest—far from it. This is letting people remember."[67] In 2012 politicians asked Tent Embassy members not to march again, but they did; again, bystanders applauded them. In 2015, though—the centenary of the Gallipoli landings—police refused to let the marchers proceed.[68]

While the debate over memorializing the frontier wars has no end in sight, two observations are clear: (1) commemorating Aboriginal and Torres Strait Islander contributions to military service has opened a new space to discuss the topic and (2) Indigenous Australians are still the ones leading the organization of commemorations through the innovative "Anzac-isation" of the frontier wars.

CONCLUSION

As this article has shown, there is a long history of commemorating Indigenous military service. This commemoration has occurred not only at official Anzac Day services and memorials but also through personal, private practices.[69] Only recently have governments and organizations like the RSL embraced the contemporary commemorations. To non-Indigenous agents of the state, military, and ex-service organizations, Aboriginal and Torres Strait Islander military service represents a story of reconciliation that may expand our conceptions of "the diggers" but does not fundamentally upset the mythology of Anzac. For Indigenous communities and their allies, though, such commemorations may serve an additional purpose. Rather than reinforcing silences about the frontier wars, this boom in commemorations of Indigenous service has opened a new, post–History Wars approach to discussing the frontier wars.

On the one hand, the boom problematizes the militarization of Australian history by destabilizing the boundaries between military history, Indigenous history, and the frontier wars. Enhancing public awareness about the frontier wars undermines much of the conservative-nationalist agenda aligned with the militarization of Australian history. On the other hand, the "Anzac-isation" of the frontier wars is arguably problematic because colonialism and dispossession continue to be viewed through a military prism. A militarized reading of the frontier wars does posit Indigenous people as defenders of Australia since time immemorial, and it does reinforce their dual identities as both Indigenous and Australian. Yet such histories potentially sideline the complex gendered and racialized power dynamics at play on the frontiers, absorbing the frontier wars into a nationalist military narrative. How Aboriginal and Torres Strait Islander communities grapple with these shifting narratives remains to be seen, but clearly they will continue to lead the charge to honor their fallen brothers and sisters.

AUTHOR BIOGRAPHY

Noah Riseman is associate professor of history at Australian Catholic University in Melbourne. He researches the history of marginalized people in the Australian military, especially Aboriginal and Torres

Strait Islander and LGBTI people. He is the coauthor of *Defending Country: Aboriginal and Torres Strait Islander Military Service since 1945* and the author of *In Defence of Country: Life Stories of Aboriginal and Torres Strait Islander Servicemen and Women* and *Defending Whose Country? Indigenous Soldiers in the Pacific War*.

NOTES

1 Liz Reed, *Bigger Than Gallipoli: War, History and Memory in Australia* (Crawley: University of Western Australia Press, 2004), 159–60.

2 Ibid., 145–51; Ken Inglis, *Sacred Places: War Memorials in the Australian Landscape*, 3rd ed. (Melbourne: Melbourne University Press, 2008), 421–22. Histories of Indigenous Australians in the Second World War include Robert Hall, *The Black Diggers: Aborigines and Torres Strait Islanders in the Second World War*, 2nd ed. (Canberra: Aboriginal Studies Press, 1997); *Fighters from the Fringe: Aborigines and Torres Strait Islanders Recall the Second World War* (Canberra: Aboriginal Studies Press, 1995); Noah Riseman, *Defending Whose Country? Indigenous Soldiers in the Pacific War* (Lincoln: University of Nebraska Press, 2012), 10–16, 35–98.

3 For a good overview of the scholarship on remembrance and the First World War, see Bart Ziino, "Introduction: Remembering the First World War Today," in *Remembering the First World War*, ed. Bart Ziino (New York: Routledge, 2015), 1–17.

4 See Murray Goot and Tim Rowse, *Divided Nation? Indigenous Affairs and the Imagined Public* (Carlton, Victoria: Melbourne University Press, 2007).

5 See Stuart Macintyre and Anna Clark, *The History Wars*, new ed. (Carlton, Victoria: Melbourne University Press, 2004).

6 Marilyn Lake and Henry Reynolds, *What's Wrong with Anzac? The Militarisation of Australian History* (Sydney: University of New South Wales Press, 2010).

7 See Henry Reynolds, *Forgotten War* (Sydney: NewSouth Publishing, 2013); John Connor, *The Australian Frontier Wars: 1788–1838* (Sydney: University of New South Wales Press, 2002); John Connor, "The Frontier War That Never Was," in *Zombie Myths of Australian Military History*, ed. Craig Stockings (Sydney: University of New South Wales Press, 2010), 10–28.

8 Inglis, *Sacred Places*, 179, 355–56.

9 "Many Served: A.I.F. Aborigines," *Reveille*, November 30, 1931, 22; "A.I.F. Aborigines: N.S.W.," *Reveille*, January 31, 1932, 20.

10 Anzac Day is Australia's national day commemorating military service. It falls on April 25 to commemorate the landing of the ANZACs (Australian and New Zealand Army Corps) at Gallipoli on April 25, 1915. It solidified as the key date of commemoration in the mid-1920s. See Carolyn Holbrook, *Anzac: The Unauthorised Biography* (Sydney: New South Publishing, 2014). For more on the RSL's mixed record with Aboriginal veterans, see Noah Riseman, "Enduring Silences, Enduring Prejudices: Australian Aboriginal Participation in the First World War," in *Endurance and the First World War: Experiences and Legacies in New Zealand and Australia*, ed. David Monger, Sarah Murray, and Katie Pickles (Newcastle upon Tyne, U.K.: Cambridge Scholars Publishing, 2014), 192–93.

11 Inglis, *Sacred Places*, 179.

12 "Memorial to Natives: Ceremony at Point McLeay," *Adelaide News*, August 18, 1925, 9; "Point McLeay Mission Station: A Memorial Window," *Adelaide Advertiser*, August 19, 1925, 9; "Point Macleay War Heroes," *Adelaide Register*, August 19, 1925, 8; Doreen Kartinyeri, *Ngarrindjeri Anzacs* (Adelaide: Aboriginal Family History Project, South Australian Museum and Raukkan Council, 1996), 8, 11–12.

13 "Anzac Day at Palm Island," *Townsville Daily Bulletin*, April 28, 1936, 3.

14 "Cape Barren Island Memorial," *Monuments Australia*, http://monumentaustralia.org.au/themes/conflict/multiple/display/70129-cape-barren-island-war-memorial; Georgia Warner, "Black Flag in Rightful Place," *Hobart Mercury*, April 26, 2000, 7.

15 "Photograph—War Memorial on Cape Barren Island," Archives Office of Tasmania, PH30-1-6674, *LINC Tasmania*, http://catalogue.statelibrary.tas.gov.au/item/?id=PH30-1-6674.

16 "Aboriginal's Tribute," *Perth Daily News*, April 25, 1945, 6; "Swan-Feather Wreath from Aboriginal," *Adelaide News*, April 25, 1945, 3; Kartinyeri, *Ngarrindjeri Anzacs*, 11.

17 "Aboriginal Officer the Main Speaker at Wagga," *Wagga Wagga (NSW) Daily Advertiser*, April 26, 1952, 1; Christobel Mattingley, *Survival in Our Own Land: "Aboriginal" Experiences in "South Australia" since 1836*, rev. ed. (Rydalmere, New South Wales: Hodder & Stoughton, 1992), 288; "Anzac Day: Kuranda Observance," *Cairns Post*, May 6, 1952, 6.

18 "Aboriginal War Heroism Praised," *Sydney Morning Herald*, July 12, 1969, 6. See also "Aborigines Gather at Memorial," *Canberra Times*, July 12, 1969, 8; "Aborigines Ceremonies Historic," *Sydney Daily Telegraph*, July 12, 1969, 12. Photos of the event are available from State Library of New South Wales, Australian Photographic Agency, 31658–69.

19 *Ka-wayawayama: Aeroplane Dance*, produced and directed by Trevor Graham, 58 minutes, Film Australia, 1994, DVD; *No Bugles, No Drums*, produced by Debra Beattie-Burnett, directed by John Burnett, 49 minutes, Seven Emus Productions in association with Australian Television Network, 1990, videocassette.

20 Bart Ziino, "Claiming the Dead: Great War Memorials and Their Communities," *Journal of the Royal Australian Historical Society* 89, no. 2 (2003): 159. See also Jay Winter, *Sites of Memory, Sites of Mourning: The Great War in European Cultural History* (Cambridge: Cambridge University Press, 1995), 80; Alistair Thomson, *Anzac Memories: Living with the Legend*, 2nd ed. (Clayton, Victoria: Monash University Publishing, 2013), 148.

21 Graham Seal, *Inventing Anzac: The Digger and National Mythology* (St. Lucia: University of Queensland Press in association with the API Network and Curtin University of Technology, 2004), 10.

22 Jay Winter, *Remembering War: The Great War between Memory and History in the Twentieth Century* (New Haven, Conn.: Yale University Press, 2006), 36; Bruce Scates, *A Place to Remember: A History of the Shrine of Remembrance* (Cambridge: Cambridge University Press, 2009), 238–40; Joy Damousi, *Living with the Aftermath: Trauma, Nostalgia and Grief in Post-war Australia* (Cambridge: Cambridge University Press, 2001), 11–13.

23 "Aboriginal Anzac March," *Canberra Times*, March 20, 1985, 9.

24 Fiona Nicoll, *From Diggers to Drag Queens: Configurations of Australian National Identity* (Annandale, New South Wales: Pluto Press Australia, 2001), 100.

25 "Ruxton Plans to Stop Aboriginal Group March," *Canberra Times*, March 5, 1985, 3; see also Richard Broome, *Fighting Hard: The Victorian Aborigines Advancement League* (Canberra: Aboriginal Studies Press, 2015), 202.

26 Joy Damousi, *The Labour of Loss: Mourning, Memory and Wartime Bereavement in Australia* (Cambridge: Cambridge University Press, 1999), 4.

27 Darryl Wallace, interview with George Bostock, April 11, 1991, Australian Institute for Aboriginal and Torres Strait Islander Studies (AIATSIS), Canberra, BOSTOCK_G01-016549–50.

28 John Lahey, "Two Veterans Raise a Memorial to Honour Aboriginal War Dead," *Melbourne Age*, March 16, 1987, 5.

29 Wallace interview.

30 Anne Brennan, "Lest We Forget: Military Myths, Memory, and Canberra's Aboriginal and Torres Strait Islander Memorial," *Memory Connection* 1, no. 1 (2011): 36.

31 Australian War Memorial, Canberra, PR91/089, Yugambeh Aboriginal Group; "Yugambeh Aboriginal War Memorial," *Monuments Australia*, http://monument australia.org.au/themes/conflict /multiple/display/90925-yugambeh -aboriginal-war-memorial/.

32 Paul Keating, "The Redfern Park Address," December 10, 1992, in *Reconciliation: Essays on Australian Reconciliation*, ed. Michelel Grattan (Melbourne: Black Inc., 2000), 63. For more on the Reconciliation movement, see Andrew Gunstone, *Unfinished Business: The Australian Formal Reconciliation Process* (Melbourne: Australian Scholarly Publishing, 2007).

33 Cec Fisher, "Anzac Day Marching on the Gold Coast in 1993," *Koori Mail*, May 2, 2001, 9.

34 Sir William Deane, "Address by Sir William Deane, Governor General of the Commonwealth of Australia on the Occasion of the Launch of *Sacred Places: War Memorials in the Australian Landscape*," Canberra, November 17, 1998, Australian Parliamentary Library, http://parlinfo.aph.gov .au/parlInfo/search/display/display .w3p;query=Id%3A%22media /pressrel/AMUQ3%22.

35 Helen McCabe, "Build Memorials for Aborigines," *Adelaide Advertiser*, November 18, 1998, 3; Claire Harvey, "Black Wars Forgotten—Deane," *Australian*, November 18, 1998, 1; "Taking Sides in Neutrality," *Sydney Daily Telegraph*, November 19, 1998, 10; Naomi Mapstone, "New Call to Record Aboriginal Conflicts," *Canberra Times*, November 19, 1998, 3; Glen St. J. Barclay, "The Politics of War . . . and a Memorial," *Brisbane Courier-Mail*, November 20, 1998; Ruth Latukefu, F. O'Connor, and Edwina Barton, "Lest We Forget All Others," *Australian*, November 21, 1998, 18; Ewan Morris, "They, Too, Fought for Home," *Australian*, November 25, 1998, 12; Andrew Bolt, "Statues Won't Help Aborigines," *Melbourne Herald-Sun*, November 26, 1998, 18; Nicolas Rothwell, "A Black Mark in Colonial History: Memories, Memorials or Merely a Fight over the Definition of War?," *Australian*, November 30, 1998, 10. Deane's official secretary sent a letter clarifying that the governor-general never took a position on the issue: Martin Bonsey, "No Views on Black Memorial," *Sydney Daily Telegraph*, November 20, 1998, 12. Inglis also expressed his views in an opinion piece: Ken Inglis, "Lest We Forget the Local Killing Fields," *Australian*, November 19, 1998, 15.

36 See "'Show Aboriginal Battles': Call to War Memorial," *Canberra Times*, November 11, 1983, 7; Janine Macdonald, "Forgotten Soldiers of an Undeclared War,"

WICAZO SA REVIEW

SPRING 2017

Melbourne Age, November 23, 1998, 6; Tom Griffiths, "Counting the Fallen of a War without Uniforms," *Sydney Morning Herald,* December 20, 2001, 12; Matt Peacock, "War Memorial Battle over Frontier Conflict Recognition," *The 7:30 Report,* February 26, 2009, Australian Broadcasting Corporation.

37 Claire Harvey, "Veterans Condemn Black War Memorial," *Australian,* November 18, 1998, 2.

38 Claire Harvey, "RSL Backs Separate Black Wars Tribute," *Australian,* November 19, 1998, 3; "FED—Deaths in 'Black Wars' Should Be Commemorated—Inglis," *Australian Associated Press,* November 18, 1998; Michael Perry, "Calls for Aboriginal War Memorial to 'Black Wars,'" *Reuters,* November 18, 1998.

39 Lake and Reynolds, *What's Wrong with Anzac?,* 2.

40 Clemence Due, "'Lest We Forget': Creating an Australian National Identity from Memories of War," *Melbourne Historical Journal* 36 (2008): 23. See also Seal, *Inventing Anzac,* 117; Reynolds, *Forgotten War,* 237.

41 Fiona Nicoll, "War by Other Means: The Australian War Memorial and the Aboriginal Tent Embassy in National Space and Time," in *The Aboriginal Tent Embassy: Sovereignty, Black Power, Land Rights and the State,* ed. Gary Foley, Andrew Schaap, and Edwina Howell (Abingdon, U.K.: Routledge, 2014), 267.

42 Damousi, *The Labour of Loss,* 163. See also Reed, *Bigger Than Gallipoli,* 130.

43 Christopher Dore, "Howard against Black War Memorial," *Australian,* November 23, 1998, 3; "FED—Howard Rules Out Aboriginal War Memorial," *Australian Associated Press,* November 22, 1998.

44 Due, "'Lest We Forget,'" 32. The *Mabo* ruling in 1992 overturned the doctrine of terra nullius and introduced the concept of native title into Australian common law.

45 "Recognition for Unsung Heroes," *Melbourne Herald-Sun,* July 30, 1999, 12; David Mclennan, "Black Soldiers: They Were 'Fighting for Their Land,'" *Canberra Times,* July 7, 1999, 3; Nick Gentle, "Exhibition Honours Contribution of Indigenous Officers," *Canberra Times,* July 30, 1999, 3.

46 Thomson, *Anzac Memories,* 247.

47 Eloise Dortch and Minh Lam, "Marchers Break New Ground," *West Australian* (Perth), April 26, 2001, 5. See also Carol Altmann, "Pride of One Day of the Year," *Australian,* April 26, 2001, 3; "Faces of Anzac Day," *Australian,* April 26, 2001, 2; "Aboriginal Pride to the Fore in Anzac Day March," *Koori Mail,* May 2, 2001, 1, 11; *The Forgotten,* directed by Glen Stasiuk, originally aired as an episode of *Message Stick* on the Australian Broadcasting Corporation (ABC), April 27, 2003, videocassette.

48 John Schnaars, interview with Noah Riseman, Perth, November 23, 2010, ORAL TRC 6260/1, National Library of Australia (hereafter NLA); "The Last Post," *Message Stick,* directed by Adrian Wells, produced by the Australian Broadcasting Corporation, 2006, DVD; Honouring Indigenous War Graves Inc., http://www.hiwg2005.websyte.com.au/site.cfm?/hiwg2005/.

49 Paul Bibby, "It's Been a Long Walk: Blacks Unite for March," *Sydney Morning Herald,* April 17, 2007. See also "NSW: Cheers and Tears for Anzac Day in NSW," *Australian Associated Press,* April 25, 2007.

50 Paul Bibby, "Redfern Turns Out for Indigenous Diggers," *Sydney Morning Herald,* April 26, 2007. See

also "NSW: Indigenous Servicemen to Be Remembered," *Australian Associated Press*, April 23, 2008; Miriam Hall, "Indigenous Prisoners of War in Focus for ANZAC Day," *PM*, ABC Radio, April 24, 2013, http://www.abc.net.au/pm/content/2013/s3744649.htm.

51 "Indigenous Veterans Commemoration Ceremony," http://www.rslnsw.org.au/uploads/IndigVetCommCer.pdf.

52 Harry Allie, interview with Noah Riseman, November 4, 2011, Chesterfield, New South Wales.

53 "Yirrkala War Memorial," *Monument Australia*, http://monument australia.org.au/display/80262-yirrkala-war-memorial; "Call to Duty with Honour," *Hobart Mercury*, November 12, 1999, 7; "Qld—Torres Strait War Memorial Planned," *Australian Associated Press*, September 30, 2000; "SA—Narungga War Veterans Honoured in Memorial," *Australian Associated Press*, November 13, 1999; "Memorial on Heritage List," *Perth Sunday Times*, April 25, 2010, Street, p. 8; Minh Lam, "Governor Calls for a Fair Go," *West Australian*, July 2, 2001, 9; Alex Sinnott, "Indigenous Servicemen Honoured," *Warrnambool Standard*, November 1, 2010, http://www.standard.net.au/story/785897/indigenous-servicemen-honoured/; Elliana Lawford, "World War II Hero Matthias Ulungura Honoured with Statue on Bathurst Island," *ABC News*, July 2, 2016, http://www.abc.net.au/news/2016-06-24/war-hero-matthias-ulungura-honoured-with-statue/7542520.

54 "Reconciliation Action Plan 2011–2015," *Department of Veterans' Affairs*, http://www.dva.gov.au/i-am/aboriginal-andor-torres-strait-islander/reconciliation-action-plan-2011-2015; "Fed: Thousands Gather in Canberra for Dawn Service," *Australian Associated Press*, April 25, 2004; "The Aboriginal and Torres Strait Islander Commemorative Ceremony," *Australian*

War Memorial, https://www.awm.gov.au/commemoration/anzac/atsivsaa/.

55 "'I Am the Forgotten Soldier': The Aboriginal and Torres Strait Islander War Memorial Appeal. Torrens Parade Ground," brochure, undated. See also Greg Kelton, "Memorial to Honour Indigenous Diggers," *Adelaide Advertiser*, May 29, 2008, State, p. 14; *For Love of Country*, directed by Malcolm McKinnon, produced by Reconciliation South Australia, 19 minutes, 2011, DVD.

56 Frank Lampard, "Dedication of the War Memorial on Torrens Parade Ground on Sunday 10 November 2013," provided to author courtesy of Frank Lampard.

57 See *Aboriginal and Torres Strait Islander Dedicated Memorial Committee Queensland*, http://atsidmcq.com/.

58 "Yininmadyemi—Thou didst let fall," *City Art Sydney*, http://www.cityartsydney.com.au/artwork/yininmadyemi-thou-didst-let-fall/; Melanie Kembrey, "Tony Albert's 'Confronting' Tribute to Indigenous Diggers Unveiled in Sydney's Hyde Park," *Sydney Morning Herald*, March 31, 2015 http://www.smh.com.au/entertainment/art-and-design/tony-alberts-confronting-tribute-to-indigenous-diggers-unveiled-in-sydneys-hyde-park-20150331-1mbuzo.html; Helen Davidson, "Indigenous War Memorial: Design Unveiled in Sydney's Hyde Park," *Guardian Australia*, November 8, 2013, http://www.theguardian.com/world/2013/nov/08/war-memorial-indigenous-soldiers-design-project.

59 Winter, *Remembering War*, 140.

60 Reynolds, *Forgotten War*, 6.

61 See *Awaken: Legend and Legacy*, National Indigenous Television, April 22, 2015; *Awaken*, National Indigenous Television, April 12, 2013; Timothy Bottoms, "Why We Ought to Be Remembering

the Frontier Wars on Anzac Day," *Melbourne Age*, April 23, 2015, http://www.theage.com.au /comment/why-we-ought-to -be-remembering-the-frontier -wars-on-anzac-day-20150423 -1mrwtp.html.

62 "2015—Redfern ANZAC Day March & Commemorative Service," http://veterans.nsw .gov.au/centenary-activity/2015 -redfern-aboriginal-anzac-day -commemoration/. See also Brennan, "Lest We Forget," 42.

63 *Yininmadyemi—Thou didst let fall.*

64 Liza-Marie Syron, "'Addressing a Great Silence': *Black Diggers* and the Aboriginal Experience of War," *New Theatre Quarterly* 31, no. 3 (2015): 226.

65 Elizabeth Furniss, "Timeline History and the Anzac Myth: Settler Narratives of Local History in a North Australian Town," *Oceania* 71, no. 4 (2001): 289.

66 Nicoll, "War by Other Means," 278–79.

67 Ibid., 281.

68 "Indigenous Protest Seeking 'Frontier Wars' Recognition Shut Down by Police, Say Organisers," *SBS News*, April 25, 2015, http:// www.sbs.com.au/news/article /2015/04/25/indigenous-protest -seeking-frontier-wars-recognition -shut-down-police-say.

69 These are outside the scope of this article, but see Bruce Scates, *Anzac Journeys: Returning to the Battlefields of World War II* (Melbourne: Cambridge University Press, 2013), 249–52; *Return to Gallipoli: Walking the Battlefields of the Great War* (Cambridge: Cambridge University Press, 2006), 202–4; Reed, *Bigger Than Gallipoli*, 132–33.

Māori as "Warriors" and "Locals" in the Private Military Industry

Maria Bargh and Quentin Whanau

T he private military industry has expanded rapidly since the 1980s and traverses many countries, governments, and peoples. Unlike other peoples described as "warrior peoples" or "martial races," Māori are not predominantly seen and do not predominantly speak about themselves as "warriors" in the private military industry, which has expanded since the 1990s. Is this a result of the image of Māori as warriors being histori- cally qualified by the accompanying image of Māori as "noble savages" who were allegedly capable of being civilized and assimilated? We sug- gest that Māori do not describe themselves as a warrior or martial race in the industry because there are other peoples in the industry who are labeled, and who label themselves, in that way, and we investigate the reasons Māori may want to differentiate themselves.

Second, we examine the idea of Māori being experts at engaging with "locals" (Indigenous peoples) in other countries. The perception of Māori in the New Zealand Defence Force is that they have a par- ticular expertise at engaging with the Indigenous peoples of countries outside New Zealand. In the private military industry, where people of many nationalities are contracted to provide military activities in coun- tries such as Iraq, non–New Zealanders view the ability to engage well with Indigenous peoples as a Kiwi (New Zealander) trait and not spe- cifically a Māori trait.[1] Māori in the private military industry describe their abilities to engage well with locals as both a Kiwi trait that they share with some of their Pākehā (New Zealanders of European descent)

SPRING 2017 WICAZO SA REVIEW

102

compatriots and as a uniquely Māori way of conducting themselves. We suggest that the sense of being good at engaging with locals as a Kiwi trait may be a result of the Māori influences on Pākehā who have served together in the New Zealand Defence Force. Māori perceptions of their own engagement with locals are bound up with Māori values of fostering successful diplomatic and working relationships through actively making connections with other peoples.

METHODOLOGY

The unique methodology of this project has been significant in the way the material has been compiled, analyzed, and presented in this article. While conducting interviews for a book project about Māori in the private military industry, I (Maria Bargh) noted that a number of interviewees made reference to long-standing assumptions about Māori as warriors and as easily able to engage with local peoples of other ethnicities. I began to wonder if these references were being used in the same way as they had been in colonial times by early British colonizers. I also wondered if the references were being used in the same way by Māori as they were by non-Māori in the private military industry. Were these comments a product of their common use in the New Zealand Defence Force and due to the fact that the interviewees trained in the New Zealand Defence Force? Or were they partially a result of that but also a reflection of rhetoric and thinking in the private military industry?

Very little is written about Māori in the private military industry beyond newspaper articles.[2] With my background in researching politics, international relations, and Māori studies I knew that answering questions about Māori sentiments of their involvement in the private military industry would require collaboration with someone who had worked in that industry. In order to work through the complexity of this issue, I began a dialogue with Quentin Whanau, who is Māori, has a background in the New Zealand Defence Force, has taught New Zealand Defence Force doctrine, and has worked in the private military industry. This article is in part an illustration of the ways that the two of us read the articulations of Māori in the New Zealand Defence Force and private military industry. Our project to bring two different perspectives together necessarily involved trying to engage and mediate between different ways of thinking about being Māori. We found a way to talk through these issues, and this negotiation is a useful method for thinking and writing across different viewpoints. The method here partially follows what Māori education academic Russell Bishop has described as "interviews as collaborative storying," whereby Quentin and I engage in the collaborative construction of new meanings by entering into a conversation from two quite different subject positions.[3] At times the conversation, and therefore this article, has relied heavily on Quentin's extensive experience in these areas, which is illustrated in substantial quotes from Quentin in this article, and has then been contrasted with published academic and New Zealand Defence Force documentation.

Bringing our two different understandings together to analyze depictions of Māori as warriors and locals provides a picture of how these ideas have been used in different ways over the years. Māori articulations of these ideas indicate a reappropriation of the terms "warriors" and "locals" from colonial applications for reuse in multiple ways—including for Māori advantage. We hope that providing a dialogical approach to analyzing how these ideas are produced and reproduced will encourage a focus on the many roles of Māori in the military and private military industry.

This research used Kaupapa Māori methodology, which is primarily for Māori and by Māori and is underpinned by a number of ethical values.[4] The values of *manaakitanga* (hosting, sharing, and generosity), *mana* (dignity), and *mahaki* (humility) were central to our research.[5] We sought to treat the different information that we brought to the dialogue with respect and care and to ensure that our robust exchanges maintained the *mana* of the material, of the people we were discussing, and of each other as cocollaborators. As a result, substantial quotations from Quentin in the latter part of the article are deliberately allowed to speak on their own terms, rather than being reinterpreted from an academic viewpoint.

Our first task was to take note of when the ideas of Māori as warriors and locals were used. The intention here is not to seek to prove whether these ideas about Māori are "true" in and of themselves; this perception will vary according to people's histories and circumstances. Our interest is what we can learn from examining how and when these ideas are used.

MĀORI AS WARRIORS

The categorization and ranking of societies, according to those who are allegedly more civilized than others, have been around for hundreds of years.[6] When the British and other Europeans encountered Indigenous peoples they made particular kinds of assumptions about these peoples and ranked their societies.[7] The categorizations by the British then went a step further to make assumptions, and subsequently a martial race theory, about particular peoples as having innate warrior or martial characteristics.[8] This process has been most commonly examined in India and Pakistan.[9]

The categorization of Māori as having a predominantly warrior culture stems from early contact between Māori and non-Māori and has been well documented.[10] Historian Franchesca Walker has described the way that the British used the assumptions of Māori as a martial race during the New Zealand Wars of the mid-1800s: "A dichotomy was formed between the civilized, intelligent warfare pursued by British troops and the 'lower' form of war waged by Māori. One newspaper highlighted this key difference during the wars, distinguishing between the groups' approach to battle: 'A Māori is a fighting animal, while the British soldier is a fighting machine. . . . One fought by instinct, the other by rule.'"[11] Walker found that during the subsequent world wars, non-Māori and Māori employed martial race discourse. Māori used it in order to add legitimacy to calls for political and economic equality, and in 1942 Apirana Ngata famously described Māori participation as warriors in the Second World War as "the price of citizenship" to the new Pākehā settler state.[12]

Since the 1980s the notion has been reiterated on various occasions and in particular ways.[13] The most prominent agency within New Zealand that consistently describes Māori as descendants of a warrior race is the New Zealand Defence Force. In the 1990s "a concerted effort took place to affirm the concept of a bicultural partnership within the New Zealand Defence Force as a whole," and in 1994 "the Services adopted Māori names."[14] The New Zealand navy adopted the name Te Taua Moana o Aotearoa (warriors of the sea); the army, Ngāti Tūmatauenga (tribe of the God of war); and the air force, Te Tauaarangi o Aotearoa (warriors of the sky).

There were a number of reasons provided by the New Zealand Defence Force for the name changes. The first was that the use of Māori tribal identity reflected the full integration of Māori into the New Zealand Defence Force—the last Māori-only unit ceased in the 1950s. The New Zealand Defence Force stated that it was "common practice in Māoridom to use the word Tūmatauenga when referring to soldiers," and therefore with integration "it was a natural progression to formalize this integration by using the name Tūmatauenga."[15] The second reason it suggested was that the names reflected the warrior culture of Māori: "Māori are traditionally tribal warrior people. . . . [T]hey identify strongly with the warrior culture of the New Zealand Defence Force."[16] The name Ngāti Tūmatauenga is "an unprecedented fusion of Māori and European Warrior Cultures towards something ancient and timeless."[17] The third reason provided was that the name changes represented the long-term contributions Māori have made to the New Zealand Defence Force, including "participation in major conflicts of the 19th and 20th century."[18]

To explain the rationale further for its personnel, the New Zealand Defence Force makes available documentation that includes a *whakapapa* (genealogy) by listing events "leading to the New Zealand Army becoming Ngāti Tūmatauenga." The *whakapapa* begins with "Māori vs European (the Kororāreka Association—1828)." British settlers formed the Kororāreka Association in lieu of a British policing system to control settlers in the Far North of the North Island of New Zealand. It is possible that this beginning of the *whakapapa* represents the time when Māori and Pākehā were separate (military) entities, opposed to one another. The second tier of the *whakapapa* is "Māori vs European & Māori (the Armed Constabulary—1867)." This appears to indicate a merging at least of some Māori who fought alongside the Crown during the land wars of the 1860s, although other Māori were still an opposing (military) force. At this next point on the *whakapapa*, the two sides were brought together in the wars where Māori fought alongside Pākehā against third party military forces: "Boer War (1899), NZ 1st and 2nd Expeditionary Forces (1914 & 1939), Māori Pioneer BN [Battalion] (1914), Te Hokowhitu a Tū (1915), 28th Māori BN [Battalion in Second World War]."[19]

Quentin proposes that a defining moment for the New Zealand Defence Force came with the suspension of New Zealand from the alliance between Australia, New Zealand, and the United States in the 1980s. The New Zealand government had introduced a nuclear-free policy in 1987, which meant that U.S. nuclear-powered frigates could no longer visit New Zealand ports. Quentin states: "Following the exclusion, during the 1980s and 1990s the New Zealand Defence Force went through a number of restructures in order to rebrand itself as a credible defense force. Previously, the New Zealand Defence Force had leaned heavily on the U.S. for equipment and training support. Throughout this period, morale suffered, and a number of personnel left feeling disillusioned."[20]

The rebranding of the New Zealand Defence Force, Quentin says, was seen as a way forward to inject some identity and purpose back into the forces: "The concept of a bicultural partnership acknowledges both Māori and Pākehā as warriors and our shared history of warfare including achievements and losses as New Zealanders. The Māori aspect gives New Zealand its uniqueness, and the ethos and values of the New Zealand Defence Force (commitment, comradeship, courage, integrity) are similar to tribal values and virtues."[21]

Quentin's views are reiterated by the New Zealand Defence Force's "Bicultural Policy," which states that the "bicultural approach enhances the New Zealand Defence Force's: 1) military ethos; 2) fighting spirit; 3) camaraderie and behaviours; 4) unique ability to accept and engage with diverse cultures in operation settings; 5) ability to attract, recruit and retain Māori members of the Armed Forces."[22] This view has also been expressed throughout the New Zealand Defence Force. For example, in a navy presentation regarding the integration of Māori into the New Zealand Defence Force, the author argues that "the ability to practice Māori traditions enhances identity and morale within the RNZN [Royal New Zealand Navy]."[23]

One of the other reasons for having a Māori name for the New Zealand army might be that approximately 22 percent of the army (including regular force, reserves, and civilians) are Māori (19.9 percent of the navy and 6.6 percent of the air force).[24] Having a Māori name for the organization possibly indicates that the services are for Māori. For the army, which has struggled to recruit and retain personnel over the past decades, appealing to people's identity may be one part of the solution.

In other countries, the timing of militaries encouraging the enlisting and serving of nonmajority populations has reflected the short- to medium-term needs of the military. In Canada, the traditional demographic of the military has been people of European descent, and the numbers of those people enlisting in the military are declining. As a result, a new discourse has begun to emerge within the Canadian forces about the military's need to reflect the ethnic diversity of the population; therefore, its focus has turned to encouraging minority groups to enlist.[25] Defense studies scholar Grazia Scoppio has compared the ways that Aboriginal Canadians and Māori have been integrated into the militaries of Canada and New Zealand. She argues that such integration has been more successful in New Zealand because of the legacies of what she describes as Māori warrior culture and the inclusion of Māori cultural practices within the New Zealand Defence Force.[26]

The use of the *haka* (dance) and *kapa haka* (performances/songs) and the construction of an army *marae* (meetinghouse) are examples of the inclusion of Māori cultural practices.[27] *Haka* has many functions; the most well known, however, is its use in Māori battles long before colonization as a psychological weapon.[28] The use of *haka* by Māori in the New Zealand Defence Force even before the First World War was a Māori initiative. The introduction of *kapa haka* and the construction of the first navy *marae* at Devonport in 2000 is described in an internal navy presentation about Māori integration as "able to embrace both the Māori and military cultures of the Royal New Zealand Navy. . . . It is a memorial to our forebears and a beacon for those yet to come."[29] *Kapa haka* is seen by many Māori as an avenue to maintain cultural traditions and Māori language, while the *marae* plays an important role for Māori, as traditionally the meetinghouse was the location for discussion political, cultural, and social matters.[30] The first army *marae* was built in Waiouru in 1995.

These are some of the ways, in internal New Zealand Defence Force presentations and documents, that the idea of Māori as a warrior people has been used within the organization, but what about in the private military industry? A number of scholars have explored the ways the private military industry is utilizing the notion of martial races. Scholar Paul Higate, for instance, has examined the ways that Fijian contractors are constructed as "members of a martial race, with lines of continuity reaching back to the intervention of the imperial powers who, mirroring the Kamba tribe in Kenya, recruited into the British army 'believed that certain sections of their subject populations had inherent combative and militaristic qualities that made them naturally suited for military service.'"[31] Gender studies scholar Amanda Chisholm has conducted research into the concept of a martial race with Gurkhas in the private military industry. Gurkhas are Nepalese soldiers who historically had a unit in the nineteenth-century British army and are commonly referred to as members of a martial race. As Chisholm discovered, Gurkhas express pride in their identity as a martial race; however, they have complained that private military and security companies exploit this reputation for an economic gain that is not adequately repaid to Ghurkha employees.[32]

From his experiences in the private military industry, Quentin argues that "Gurkhas were more commonly identified as warrior people than Māori. When people said, 'He's a Gurkha,' it meant a whole association with warriorness: a good fighter, very disciplined and professional. If people say, 'He's Nepalese,' it doesn't mean anything, but if you say, 'He's a Gurkha,' that's different." There is an implication of a ranking of peoples according to their apparent "warriorness."

Although Māori share a historical discourse of being descendants of a warrior race with the Gurkhas and Fijians, this appears to not be widely known in the private military industry. Quentin suggests that while Gurkhas and Fijians have a clear reputation as warrior people, Māori are not perceived in quite the same way:

> Māori don't have a reputation, because we're usually
> lumped in as Kiwis. We're identified as New Zealanders,
> not as an individual race. So, for example, when they talk
> about an operator who's doing a really good job, they see
> him as a New Zealander first, and then if he has a Māori
> name, then he is identifiable as Māori. We are identifiable
> as different from other Kiwis because of our Māori names.
> There are, of course, also Māori with European names,
> and then it wouldn't be until it is brought to an outsider's
> attention—that person is Māori.

In large part, this perception of Māori as predominantly Kiwis may be a result of American companies dominating the private military industry and their limited knowledge of Māori.[33] Quentin explains:

> The Americans don't really know about Māori. It's only
> through recent conflicts where we've fought side by side
> with them that they realize Māori make up a significant
> part of the defense force. In the private military industry

it might be their first contact with a Māori. At one time there were two Māori guys who worked in security at the U.S. Embassy in the Green Zone, Iraq. From working with Americans and through work association, then some Americans knew who Māori were. Māori were noticeably different from other Kiwis because they had either a first or last name that was Māori and they had to teach people how to pronounce it. Māori were often confused with Hispanics, possibly because the other big group of brown people that the Americans know are Hispanics. Brits were a bit different. They know us by culture. There's been a close association since they colonized us. Those Brits who were in the private military industry that had served in the military with New Zealanders knew more about Māori as warrior descendants.

Why is it that while Gurkhas and Fijians are treated as marital races in the private military industry, Māori are not, despite coming from similar discursive contexts about warriors? Does it have something to do with the other images associated with Māori? One of the other dimensions of Māori being described as a martial race is the accompanying assumption about the potential for Māori to be civilized.

The use of the image of Māori as noble savages has been subtler in the 1990s and 2000s than the warrior image, and the term is not now used explicitly. Many early British settlers to New Zealand understood Māori as being both of a warrior culture and a noble savage because Māori cultivated the land and showed a keen interest in commerce.[34] According to Adam Smith and others who adhered to the theory of stages of history, if societies showed signs of cultivation or commerce, then they were at a more advanced level of civilization than, say, those who "hunted and gathered."[35] As scholar Michaela Moura-Koçoğlu also points out, Māori were deemed noble savages in the 1800s because they were seen as "amenable both to civilisation and to survival" and as "superior to the Natives of the 'new world.'"[36]

Although British settlers in the 1800s perceived Māori as having an inherent savagery (as manifested in their warriorness), they were also perceived as being able to be trained and assimilated, supposedly placing them slightly higher than the average "savage" on the hierarchy of humanity.[37] The population may be noble and one step above the savagery of others, but still at heart Māori were savage and therefore could not be entirely trusted by British colonizers to manage their own Māori affairs.[38]

Some of these kinds of views about Māori could explain the different treatment of Māori from other peoples categorized as martial races when it comes to management positions in the private military industry. Quentin suggests that the role that race and ethnicity play in selection criteria for management or other senior positions in the private military industry is not always overt or transparent:

> There are unofficial selection criteria for management positions. Fijians are seen as good fighters. Gurkhas and Fijians stand out. There are guard forces that are entirely one of those. However, they never really occupied management positions, but Māori were sometimes headhunted for management positions because we're seen as being "smart buggers"! Māori are seen as more intelligent and independent. The other aspect of this is that many of those guard forces that were entirely Fijian or Gurkha didn't tend to mix with their generally white supervisors, whereas because of their management positions Māori did mingle with other team leaders. I've never seen a Gurkha or Fijian out of their group. They tend to stick with their own. Māori are seen as able to assimilate. We're seen as having been assimilated into Kiwi / New Zealand identity.

MĀORI AS LOCALS

In interviews I conducted in 2013 and 2014 (and subsequently published) with Māori serving in the private military industry, interviewees made numerous comments about the distinctive nature of Māori (and often by association of Kiwis) in the private military industry.[39] Interviewees suggested that Māori have more of an ability to relate to and empathize with local (Indigenous) peoples in whichever country they are operating because of shared experiences of colonization, occupation, and being Indigenous peoples. This idea of Māori as being able to bond and identify easily with locals (Indigenous peoples) in a place is one that is commonly discussed in the New Zealand Defence Force, particularly with regard to Māori deployed in the Pacific.

In 1997–98 the New Zealand Defence Force deployed peacekeeping operations in Bougainville in response to the civil war between Bougainville and Papua New Guinea and to East Timor in 1999 as part of INTERFET after the East Timorese voted to become independent from Indonesia.[40] The New Zealand Defence Force often presents the peacekeeping operations in Bougainville and East Timor as success stories in large part because of the presence of Māori soldiers and Māori cultural practices. Some have described Māori *tikanga* (cultural practices) and protocols as being the key part of New Zealand peacekeeping in those places, with the *kapa haka* often mentioned as also essential.[41] In relation to the New Zealand peacekeepers being sent to Bougainville in 1997–98, the commander of the coalition, Brig. Roger Mortlock, stated that "the

Māori concert group and a good shipment of guitars are going to be the main weapons in our arsenal."[42] Others argued that in Bougainville, "Māori are highly respected."[43] Rhys Puddicombe from the Australian Department of Foreign Affairs, who joined the Truce Monitoring Group, noted, "The New Zealand military was heavily weighted with Māori who had instant and close empathy with Bougainvilleans. The predominance of Māori officers and soldiers was a deliberate and very effective choice."[44]

In the private military industry, non–New Zealanders perceived this trait of being able to engage with locals easily as a Kiwi way of doing things, rather than as something specific to Māori. Quentin stated,

> In the private military industry, people don't generally comment directly to you about how you do things and if they recognize it as a "Kiwi way" or not, but you hear from others. One of the general comments I heard about us is that Kiwis are seen to be more friendly with the locals and too trusting of locals who are working in their teams. Most of the Western guys had a more reserved attitude toward locals in their teams and only really trusted other expats [expatriates], particularly in situations that involved conflict. Once when I was a team leader, my driver told me that if anything happened, the team would look after me because of the way I treated them and interacted with them. I took that to mean the Kiwi/Māori way I interacted them. Some of the other Pākehā guys shared similar views and experiences.

Despite the perception from other people of the way Māori interacted in the private military industry as being a Kiwi trait, Māori themselves in the industry described aspects of engaging with locals as being uniquely Māori and bound up with Māori legal and social values of building working relationships and alliances through actively making connections with other peoples. Quentin argued, "In places where Māori and Indigenous peoples have things in common like religion, family, histories of colonization, this enables you to bond with each other. The perception from locals in places like Iraq was that generally white or expat colleagues predominantly think they're superior. When Māori are in charge, say, as team leaders, they have a different approach to creating a working environment. The white or expat colleagues base their methods more on the carryover from colonial times, whereas Māori aim for a more inclusive approach." Making connections and highlighting commonalities, Quentin indicated, is philosophically *whakawhanaungatanga*, a Māori way of building and maintaining any good relationships with other peoples. "In every country I worked in," Quentin recalls, regardless of whether English was spoken, I always took the time to learn some basic phrases to help bond with locals. They were only too happy to teach you new words and phrases daily and would test your retention randomly. I suspect this was their way of determining how genuine you were about learning their culture. As a Māori, food plays an important cultural role in connecting with people. I love food and would jump at an opportunity to experience local food. It was a great way to bond with locals in a relaxed setting. Being invited to share a meal was always an experience, but not everyone was keen to try the local food, for reasons ranging from "I don't trust it!" to "I hate the food!" Some colleagues (mostly U.S./Brits/Australians) would make excuses not to participate or to eat with locals, which I thought was insensitive and I'm sure the locals regarded as disrespectful. These types of attitudes did nothing to help build relationships with locals.

By trying to engage with local people by spending time with them and participating in informal rituals of connection like sharing food, Māori were building working relationships and bonds with those people.

Quentin describes showing an interest in history as another means of connecting with locals: "Taking the time to learn about the history and culture of the people helped build an understanding of them, and in return it was an opportunity to share things about my own culture. From my experience, Indigenous people are very good at reading body language and can tell if you're genuine or not. Being Māori you definitely relate to other Indigenous peoples in regard to colonization—shared experiences certainly resonate with you regardless of nationality." Quentin notes that for some Māori who looked like the locals, the Indigenous peoples of those places, that also provided an opportunity for bonding—and mistaken identity. "One time," Quentin says, "in Afghanistan I was at a meeting, and some local Hazara people were trying to talk to me, and the interpreter picked it up, because he saw them staring at me when I didn't respond. He managed to explain to them that I wasn't being rude—I just wasn't Hazara." In my aforementioned interviews with other Māori in the private military industry, I also recorded comments that support Quentin's perspective.[45] One of them, T, suggested, "It's not so much being 'a Māori' that gives you a point of difference; rather, it's being brought up 'as Māori' that may be of assistance to getting work or helping you in your work, especially when working in foreign countries where locals don't speak English and don't share recognisable customs and beliefs. You learn that different groups of people have different *kawa* [cultural practices usually relating to formal procedures at a meetinghouse] and *tikanga* [correct procedures and customs] relating to everyday activities, and you learn to be respectful of those differences."[46] The sense of connection that Quentin articulates reflects Māori values and concepts of *whakapapa* (genealogy) and *whakawhanaungatanga* (fostering family connections). *Whakapapa* and *whakawhanaungatanga* were central aspects of Māori legal and social traditions in which relationships with others were crucial in political and economic interactions.[47] By using Māori cultural practices like *kapa haka* and/or Māori language, Māori in the private military industry are to some extent reasserting those traditional Māori concepts in new ways and in different settings.

CONCLUSION

This article has explored how the interconnected ideas of Māori as warriors and as locals or Indigenous peoples are articulated from the New Zealand Defence Force and through the private military industry. We have argued that, unlike other peoples described as martial races, Māori are not predominantly seen and do not often speak about themselves as a martial race in the private military industry. We suggested that this is a result of the image of Māori as warriors being historically qualified by the accompanying image of Māori as noble savages who are capable of being civilized and assimilated. We argued Māori do not describe themselves as a martial race in the industry because there are other peoples labeled in that way, namely, the Gurkhas and Fijians.

The private military industry popularly perceives Māori engagement with locals as a Kiwi trait. Although in some instances Māori have agreed with their inclusion in this Kiwi identity, some also described their connections with local Indigenous peoples as a uniquely Māori feature. Building diplomatic and working relationships by actively making connections with other peoples has long been a key feature of Māori practices relating to *whakapapa* and *whakawhanaungatanga*.

We suggest that research on Māori and other Indigenous peoples in the private military industry needs to be attentive to the multiple ways that Indigenous peoples actively renegotiate colonial perceptions of them. Much of the critical scholarship on the private military industry is conducted from afar or focuses on structural inequalities or racialization in the industry.[48] It might be useful for this research to be cautious and not to assume too much, to generalize about those peoples in the industry, or to skim over their agency in the industry.

Although this article has focused primarily on the perspectives and experiences of one individual and is therefore tentative in its findings, it could be appropriate for researchers in the field to consider that just because a group of people has been defined as a martial race in colonial discourses and in the military does not automatically mean this will continue to be the case in the private military industry. The political and cultural context and dynamics amongst the actors in the private military industry can change how peoples are perceived. One of the ways that we have suggested might assist in foregrounding the complex roles of Indigenous peoples is by engaging in collaborative storytelling or dialogues between those with experiences in the industry and those from outside it.

GLOSSARY

Aotearoa. One of the Māori names for New Zealand.
haka. Performance.
kapa haka. Performances/songs.
kaupapa Māori. Issues pertaining to Māori.
kawa. Māori procedures and protocols, usually pertaining to the *marae.*
mahaki. Humility.
mana. Authority.
manaakitanga. Hosting, sharing, and demonstrating generosity.
marae. Meeting place / meetinghouse.
Ngāti Tūmatauenga. The New Zealand army's Māori name.
Pākehā. A New Zealander of European descent.
Te Reo. The Māori language.
tikanga. Māori cultural practices. Also used to describe Māori legal
    principles.
Tūmatauenga. The god of war.
whakapapa. Genealogy.
whakawhanaungatanga. Fostering relationships with family.
whānau. Family.

AUTHORS' BIOGRAPHIES

Maria Bargh is from the Te Arawa and Ngāti Awa Māori tribes and is senior lecturer in Māori studies at Victoria University of Wellington, New Zealand. She researches and teaches in the areas of Māori politics, the Māori economy, and resource management. Her most recent publication is *A Hidden Economy: Māori in the Privatised Military Industry.*

Quentin Whanau is from the Te Atiawa Māori tribe. He has served in the New Zealand military and has worked in the private security industry.

NOTES

1 A kiwi is a flightless bird that is endemic to New Zealand. It is also used, however, by many New Zealanders as a nickname to describe people who are from New Zealand, and its usage dates back to military contexts before the First World War.

2 See, for example, P. Charman, "Kiwi Sees Fighting Off Pirates as Just a Job," *New Zealand Herald*, July 20, 2013, http://www.nzherald.co.nz/nz/news/article.cfm?c_id=1&objectid=10900435; L. Cleave, "Kiwi in Iraq Died Doing Work He Loved," *New Zealand Herald*, July 13, 2007, http://www.nzherald.co.nz/nz/news/article.cfm?c_id=1&objectid=10451295; Staff Reporters, "Ex-SAS Men in Secret Rescue," *New Zealand Herald*, March 9, 2000, http://www.nzherald.co.nz/nz/news/article.cfm?c_id=1&objectid=124856.

3 Russell Bishop, "Interviewing as Collaborative Storytelling," *Education, Research and Perspectives* 24, no. 1 (1997): 28–47.

4 Linda T. Smith, *Decolonizing Methodologies* (London: Zed Books, 1999).

5 Fiona Cram, "Rangahau Māori: Tōna Tika, Tōna Pono—the Validity and Integrity of Māori Research," in *Research Ethics in Aotearoa / New Zealand*, ed. Martin Tolich (Auckland: Longman, 2001), 35–54.

6 Barry Hindess, "Unintended Rhetoric: The 'Little Children Are Sacred' Report," in *Studies in Australian Politics Rhetoric*, ed. John Uhr and Ryan Walter (Canberra: ANU Press, 2014), 87.

7 Barry Hindess, "The Past Is Another Culture," *International Political Sociology* 1, no. 4 (2007): 325–38.

8 Cynthia Enloe, *Ethnic Soldiers: State Security in a Divided Society* (Middlesex: Penguin, 1980).

9 Heather Streets, *Martial Races* (Manchester: Manchester University Press, 2004).

10 See Brendan Hokowhitu, "Tackling Maori Masculinity: A Colonial Genealogy of Savagery and Sport," *Contemporary Pacific* 16, no. 2 (2004): 259–84; Franchesca Walker, "'Descendants of a Warrior Race': The Māori Contingent, the Pioneer Battalion and the Martial Race Myth 1914–1919," *War and Society* 31, no. 1 (2012): 7–8; Michelle Erai, "Māori Soldiers: Māori Experiences of the New Zealand Army," (master's thesis, Victoria University of Wellington, 1995).

11 Walker, "'Descendants of a Warrior Race,'" 7–8.

12 Ibid.

13 In other nonmilitary areas, the notion of Māori as warrior-like continues to emerge, including in popular culture, such as the novel and movie *Once Were Warriors*. Some scientists have claimed to have discovered a "warrior gene," which they suggested Māori embodied. A number of articles subsequently criticized the research on scientific grounds. See R. Lea and G. Chambers, "Monoamine Oxidase, Addiction, and the 'Warrior' Gene Hypothesis," *New Zealand Medical Journal* 120, no. 1,250 (2007); G. R. Hook, "Warrior Genes and the Disease of Being Māori," *MAI Review* 2 (2009), http://www.review.mai.ac.nz/index.php/MR/article/view/222/243; T. Merriman and V. Cameron, "Risk-Taking: Behind the Warrior Gene Story," *New Zealand Medical Journal* 120, no. 1 (2007): 250.

14 Author unknown, "The Integration of Māori into the New Zealand Defence Force," New Zealand navy presentation paper provided by New Zealand Defence Force personnel to the authors in hard copy only, undated.

15 New Zealand Defence Force, *Ngāti Tūmatauenga Book One*, internal New Zealand Defence Force document for army personnel outlining the history of the adoption of the name Ngāti Tūmatauenga, undated, 5.

16 Author unknown, "The Integration of Māori."

17 Col. E. G. Williams, "The New Zealand National Army Marae 20 Year Celebration," *Army News* 455 (August 2014): 8.

18 New Zealand Defence Force, *Ngāti Tūmatauenga Book One*, 6.

19 Ibid.

20 Quentin Whanau, in dialogue with Maria Bargh, January 2015, Wellington.

21 Ibid.

22 New Zealand Defence Force, "Bicultural Policy," in *Defence Force Orders 3, Part 5: Understanding the New Zealand Defence Force Workplace Environment*, chap. 5, version 17/12 (2012), 7.

23 Author unknown, "The Integration of Māori."

24 "Armed Forces," in *Te Ara Encyclopedia of New Zealand*, http://www .teara.govt.nz/en/graph/35716 /defence-force-personnel-by -gender-and-ethnicity-2012. Te Puni Kōkiri put the numbers of Māori in the army at 20 percent in 2008.

25 Jan Hilario, "Searching for Diversity in the Canadian Forces," *Source Forum of Diversity* 12, no. 25 (2012), http://thelasource.com /en/2012/03/09/searching-for -diversity-in-the-canadian-forces/.

26 Grazia Scoppio, "Indigenous Peoples in the New Zealand Defence Force and Canadian Forces," *Canadian Military Journal* 10, no. 4 (2007), http://www.journal.forces .gc.ca/vol10/no4/07-scoppio-eng .asp.

27 A *marae* is a meeting place where, in traditional times and today, political discussions are held and cultural knowledge is transmitted.

28 Nathan Matthews and Karyn Paringatai, "Ngā mahi a Tāne-rore me te Rēhia," in *Ki te Whaiao: An Introduction to Māori Culture and Society*, ed. T. Ka'ai, J. Moorfield,

M. O'Reilly, and S. Mosley (Auckland: Pearson, 2004), 106.

29 Author unknown, "The Integration of Māori."

30 Matthews and Paringatai, "Ngā mahi a Tāne-rore me te Rēhia."

31 Paul Higate, "Martial Races and Enforcement Masculinities of the Global South: Weaponising Fijian, Chilean and Salvadoran Postcoloniality in the Mercenary Sector," *Globalizations* 9, no. 1 (2012): 43.

32 Amanda Chisholm, "The Silenced and Indispensible," *International Feminist Journal of Politics* 16, no. 1 (2013): 26–47.

33 P. W. Singer, *Corporate Warriors: The Rise of the Privatized Military Industry*, 2nd ed. (Ithaca, N.Y.: Cornell University Press, 2008).

34 Adam Smith, quoted in H. Petrie, *Chiefs of Industry* (Auckland: Auckland University Press, 2006). See also James Belich, "Myth, Race and Identity in New Zealand," *New Zealand Journal of History* 31, no. 1 (1997): 9–22.

35 Bruce Buchan, "Enlightened Histories: Civilization, War and the Scottish Enlightenment," *European Legacy* 10, no. 2 (2005): 182.

36 Michaela Moura-Koçoğlu, "From Noble Savage to Brave New Warrior," in *Literature for Our Times: Postcolonial Studies in the Twenty-First Century*, ed. B. Ashcroft, R. Mendis, J. McGonegal, and A. Mukherjee (New York: Rodopi, 2012), 371–72.

37 Barry Hindess, "The Liberal Government of Unfreedom," *Alternatives* 26 (2001): 103.

38 Barry Hindess and Christine Helliwell, "The Empire of Uniformity and the Government of Subject Peoples," *Cultural Values* 6 (2002): 139–52.

39 Maria Bargh, *A Hidden Economy: Māori in the Privatised Military*

Industry (Wellington: Huia Publishers, 2015).

40 Donald Denoon and Monica Wehner, eds., *Without a Gun: Australians' Experiences Monitoring Peace in Bougainville, 1997–2001* (Canberra: Pandanus Books, 2001); Office of the Controller and Auditor General, *New Zealand Defence Force Deployment to East Timor*, 2001, http://www.oag.govt.nz/2001/east-timor/docs/timor.pdf.

41 Tracey Haines, "An Indigenous Monitor," in Denoon and Wehner, *Without a Gun*, 109–12; and *War with No Guns*, film trailer, undated, http://www.tmipictures.co.nz/wwng.html.

42 *War with No Guns.*

43 Radio New Zealand, "Maori Highly Respected by Bougainville Leaders," June 19, 2013, http://www.radionz.co.nz/news/te-manu-korihi/138000/Māori-%27highly-respected%27-by-bougainville-leaders; Volunteer Service Abroad, "Te Wiki o Te Reo Maori, VSA Taking Kiwi Culture to the Pacific," July 2014, http://www.vsa.org.nz/blog/news/te-wiki-o-te-reo-Māori-vsa-taking-kiwi-culture-to-the-pacific/.

44 Rhys Puddicombe, "Role of the Chief Negotiator," in Denoon and Wehner, *Without a Gun*, 67.

45 Bargh, *A Hidden Economy.*

46 T is a pseudonym. All interviewees in the book selected pseudonyms, as some continue to work in the industry. T quoted in ibid., 40.

47 Hirini Mead, *Tikanga* (Wellington: Huia Publishers, 2003).

48 See, for example, Saskia Stachowitsch, "Military Privatization as a Gendered Process," in *Gender and Private Security in Global Politics*, ed. Maya Eichler (Oxford: Oxford University Press, 2015), 19–36.

Strong Hearts, Wounded Souls Revisited
The Research, the Findings, and Some Observations of Recent Native Veteran Readjustment

Tom Holm

In early 1981 my longtime friend Harold "Hodge" Barse, a Sioux/Wichita/Kiowa who was at the time a readjustment counselor with the Oklahoma City Veterans Administration Outreach program, called to ask me if I knew of any studies of Native American Vietnam veterans. I had to say that I did not know of any. With that telephone call we began an unfunded inquiry into the lives of American Indian Vietnam veterans. It was, in keeping with the foundations of American Indian studies, an activist, academic approach to what we perceived was a largely overlooked and misunderstood group of Indian people who not only deserved recognition for their military service but also merited attention to their specific needs in dealing with their return from a war zone. Both Hodge and I were veterans—he of the army, I of the Marine Corps—and very much aware of the various problems of our veterans and the social, political, and economic conditions they faced upon their homecoming. In particular, Hodge wanted to collect information on our veterans so that he, in turn, could make a case to the Readjustment Counseling Service of the then Veterans Administration to identify and deal with the specific needs of Native American veterans.[1]

HISTORY OF AND APPROACH TO RESEARCH

Very quickly we developed a one-page questionnaire and circulated it among several Native veterans we knew personally. One overwhelming notion that the few Vietnam veterans we interviewed referred to was that of being recognized for their service. Vietnam was an unpopular war, and many Native Americans opposed it because Indians were subject to the draft and could be sent to war even though the Native population in the United States was extremely poor. Moreover, the U.S. government failed to recognize Indian civil, sovereign, treaty, and human rights.[2]

Obviously, Native veterans saw their service in a different light, a conception of self that reflected their cultural values as opposed to their political views. They thought of themselves as tribal warriors, an idea that carries a meaning for Native Americans that is very different from its meaning for the larger American society. Perhaps the best way to explain the notion of warriorhood in tribal societies is to look at it in terms of relationships rather than roles. While each American Indian tribe has its own practices, there are some commonalities among many North American tribes. Traditionally, a warrior is part of a community and is not segregated in a base or camp. Members of the community view the warrior as a relative who takes part in battle not only to protect the community but also to restore justice and serve the people in other ways. The warrior may be a scout who finds resources or one who warns the community of a coming attack and becomes the first line of defense against an enemy.[3]

In 1981, when Hodge contacted me, the way to begin an organization or to ensure the recognition of certain persons or groups among Indian people in western Oklahoma was to hold a powwow. Hodge initiated such an effort at the Wichita tribal grounds near Anadarko, Oklahoma, in order to form the Vietnam Era Veterans Inter-Tribal Association and Gourd Dance Society. This powwow, held in 1981, was the first of a long series of events held in honor of Native Vietnam veterans. I was able to go to Oklahoma and lend my meager assistance in organizing that and a few more subsequent dances.

The powwow helped bring together a number of Vietnam veterans to gourd dance and thus participate in a time-honored warriors' ceremony. According to Kiowa tradition, a lone warrior who was on his journey home from a war party heard some beautiful songs. He investigated the source of the songs and found a red wolf, who taught him the songs and the ceremonies that went with the power or medicine they engendered. The origins of the gourd dance are somewhat controversial. The Kiowa people claim the ceremonies as their own based on this particular piece of their oral tradition. On the other hand, the Cheyenne Bowstring Society also claims the gourd dance as a part of the society's ceremonies. In 1838 a combined force of Comanche, Kiowa, and Apache warriors defeated the Cheyenne Bowstring warriors in the battle of Wolf Creek. It was then, according to several of William Meadows's Comanche informants, that the Comanches, Kiowas, and Apaches captured the ceremony from the Cheyennes. Whatever the origins of the dance, and however the Kiowas, Comanches, and Apaches acquired the dance, the Kiowas are undoubtedly those who revived the dance and have overseen its dispersion. The dance itself has become a prelude to the intertribal dances of powwows across the nation. It is easy to perform, and its accoutrements—the blanket, sash, rattle, and fan—are relatively inexpensive.[4]

At the same time Hodge was putting together the first Vietnam veterans' powwow, he and Frank Montour, an outreach counselor from the Detroit area, were talking their superiors in the Veterans Administration (VA) into forming a working group on American Indian Vietnam veterans. The VA had just formed a committee to look into the problems of African American and Latino veterans. The formation of the African American / Hispanic advisory committee led to the establishment of both the Readjustment Counseling Service (RCS) Working Group on American Indian Vietnam Veterans and the VA Advisory Committee on Native American Veterans. The RCS group was the first of these investigative teams formed in 1983 under the leadership of Harold Barse and Frank Montour.[5]

The RCS Working Group first addressed the problem of gathering information on Native veterans. At first we decided that we really could not conduct a random survey of Native American Vietnam veterans simply because we had no way of determining what would have been a proper sample. Instead, we chose to draw up a questionnaire and utilize our own contacts among our Native people to establish a network of veterans. The newly organized Vietnam Era Veterans Inter-Tribal Association became the starting point.

The RCS Native American group developed a questionnaire that was, unfortunately, no more and no less than a sample of convenience. There was no grand total of Native Vietnam veterans from which a random sampling could be derived. We really did not know how many Indian Vietnam veterans there actually were. One estimate from the Bureau of Indian Affairs was forty-two thousand veterans, as reported on a tribe-by-tribe basis. Complicating this matter was the question of who really was an Indian, let alone which of them were Vietnam veterans. As we discovered along the way, there were individuals who claimed to be Native Vietnam veterans but who actually were not. In consequence, we attempted to control these sampling problems by interviewing individuals at powwows and other Native gatherings and utilizing contacts in our own tribes. It did not take long to realize that the answers to our questions both in the interviews and on the questionnaire were becoming repetitive. Given that fact, as principal investigator, I decided to cut off the survey at 170 veterans, an arbitrary number but one that appeared to capture a very reasonable sense of the veterans' backgrounds, branch of service, military occupations, education levels, and combat experience.[6]

WICAZO SA REVIEW

SPRING 2017

At various intervals I published several articles on Native American Vietnam veterans and their readjustment to civilian life, the first of which was published in *Four Winds* in 1982. My articles about Native Vietnam veterans, based on accumulated data, appeared in the *Journal of Military and Political Sociology*, *Plural Societies*, *Wicazo Sa Review*, and *Armed Forces & Society* through the 1980s. These publications were in addition to the collective committee work a number of colleagues and I did for the Veterans Administration in the 1980s.[7]

The Native American Advisory Committee was established under the Consolidated Omnibus Budget Reconciliation Act of 1986. The head of this committee was Raymond C. Field, who, in turn, reported directly to the VA's administrator, Gen. Thomas Turnage. This group issued its final report on February 1, 1989, even though its work essentially had been completed a full year before. In fact, the report coincided with that of the African American / Hispanic report. The report basically concluded that Native Americans underutilized VA services and that the VA should partner with the Indian Health Services to deliver veterans' benefits, particularly in the area of health care.[8]

The RCS committee's final report was distributed in May 1992. In 1986 the working group produced a film, *Shadow of the Warrior*, which was distributed to every one of the VA medical center libraries. The film includes testimonies from American Indian Vietnam veterans to show the links between family histories, tribal warrior traditions, and cultural knowledge that could assist in healing for returned veterans.[9] In sum, the RCS Working Group found that tribal ceremonies and social/cultural traditions could, in fact, help veterans deal with the symptoms of post-traumatic stress disorder (PTSD) as defined in the third edition of the *Diagnostic and Statistical Manual of Mental Disorders (DSM-III)*.[10] This committee's final report was published in *American Indian and Alaska Native Mental Health Research: The Journal of the National Center* in 1994. Robin LaDue, Frank Montour, and I served on both working groups.[11]

Twelve years before the 1992 final report of the RCS Native American committee, there were two seminal reports on the effects of the war on Vietnam veterans. The first was the presentation of the symptomatology of PTSD in the *DSM-III*. The second was *Myths and Realities: A Study of Attitudes toward Vietnam Era Veterans*. The latter study was a Veterans Administration report submitted to the Senate Committee on Veterans' Affairs. This rather neglected study pointed out that negative attitudes toward Vietnam veterans varied from place to place across the country. Rural, tight-knit communities tended to have more positive views of the war itself and of those who experienced combat in Vietnam than the views held in urban areas, where society was more disjointed and individualized.[12]

The significance of the two VA committees on Native American veterans is that they confirm that Native veterans indeed have a high rate of PTSD symptoms and that, coming mostly from rural areas, Indians (1) were underutilizing VA services, (2) came from extended, tight-knit families that valued tribal traditions associated with both spiritual and physical well-being, (3) were from communities that valued warrior traditions over the politics of war, and (4) had, therefore, ways of dealing with PTSD that were different from and perhaps more positive than those of the dominant society. On the other hand, urban Indians tended not to have the cultural, social, and healing support systems that might have aided in their readjustment and recovery.

The Native American committees, taken together, resulted in two immediate outcomes. Don Johnson, a member of the RCS committee and an outreach counselor in Washington state; David Mann, known as Coyote; Joe Jay Pinkham; and the tribal council of the Yakama Nation started up a four-day retreat on the Yakama Reservation for veterans and Veterans Administration care givers. The retreat, known as Camp Chaparral for the place on the reservation at which it was and still is held, was planned as a therapeutic refuge for veterans and a space where VA counselors and care givers could learn about Native American ways of healing. Camp Chaparral has been maintained for over twenty years.[13] The second outcome was Senator Spark Matsunaga's (D-Hawaii) 1990 legislation, which extended the National Vietnam Veterans Readjustment Study specifically to American Indians and Native Hawai'ians.[14] Robin LaDue, who was on both the RCS and the VA Native teams, even testified on our reports before Senator Matsunaga's Veterans' Affairs Committee.

Given the level of productivity of both the VA Native American Advisory Committee and the RCS Working Group on Native American Vietnam Veterans, imagine my dismay when I discovered that the VA itself has simply ignored this rather large body of work. The Veterans Administration website plainly states that Senator Matsunaga's PL 101-507 bill was actually conceived as a result of the African American / Hispanic committee report of 1988. Moreover, PL 101-507 directed the VA's National Center for PTSD to conduct a broad study of Native American, Native Alaskan, Native Hawai'ian, and Japanese American veterans.[15]

The Native American / Alaska Native study was handed to Spero Manson, who became the head of Centers for American Indian / Alaska Native Health.[16] Since 1996 Manson and his colleagues have produced a series of articles on Native Americans and PTSD without even citing the findings of the VA's Native American Advisory Committee, any of my articles on the subject, or my 1996 book, *Strong Hearts, Wounded Souls*.[17] The center did, however, reprint the 1992 report of the RCS Working Group on American Indian Vietnam Veterans with an introduction by its director.

The woeful lack of acknowledgment of the VA advisory group

and the RCS reports on the part of the Veterans Administration essentially relegates these two productive committees to the category of government waste and neglect. Most significantly, the studies produced by Manson's Centers for American Indian / Alaska Native Health have added absolutely nothing new to the studies of American Indians and PTSD written for the RCS study by Don Johnson, Robin LaDue, Steven Silver, Harold Barse, and myself.

STRONG HEARTS, WOUNDED SOULS
REVISITED

My dismay at the neglect of the RCS Working Group on American Indian Vietnam Veterans was assuaged somewhat by the words in Frank Montour's introduction to the team's final report: "Unprepared for the sizeable response [to the survey of 170 Native vets], the group turned to Tom Holm, Ph.D., a professor at the University of Arizona and a group member. Tom became our 'keeper of words.'"[18] Frank's words were indeed an honor and an inspiration. Four years later, the University of Texas Press published *Strong Hearts, Wounded Souls*. Generally, the book received good reviews and prompted others in Native American / Indigenous peoples studies to regard me as a specialist in Native American military service.

Looking at *Strong Hearts* from the distance of over twenty years (the manuscript went through several revisions and rejections), the study brought to light the strengths of Native American communities in bringing home and socially absorbing individual veterans' war-induced trauma. The idea of "social absorption" was relatively new and raised more than a few eyebrows among psychologists who studied PTSD as a disorder that had to be worked through on an individual basis or perhaps in group therapy facilitated by trained clinicians. But after cross-tabulating the responses to the questions in the RCS survey, it became clear that the symptoms of PTSD (rage, sleep intrusions, feelings of isolation, etc.) were being worked through by those Native veterans who took part in tribal honoring or healing ceremonies. Among Native American people the maintenance of tribal identity or peoplehood is extremely important. When veterans participate in time-honored ceremonies to honor or heal, they are given valued status simply because they did their part in preserving tribal culture and, additionally, in bonding all of those who engage in such ceremonies.

There are several concepts involved in explaining the social absorption of war-related trauma. These ideas make up a complex and interwoven fabric of healing, ceremonial participation, personal and group identity, the relationships within the particular group, and what constitutes individual social status. An understanding of the healing process in many Native American societies is essential to grasping how and why Native veterans have been able to work through the problems associated with PTSD. The Western concept of medicine has, in the Greek tradition, focused on healing the body, mind, and spirit. I have discussed the path of healing in tribal societies with numerous medicine people, and I have learned that Native healers add "environment" to the Western medicine formula. The medicine of many Native American tribes attempts both to cure trauma and disease and to provide psychological help; very importantly, that same medicine also uplifts the patient's spiritual well-being and, in the larger sense, maintains his or her relationship with the spirit world.

In most Native traditions, the spirit world is part of the environment. Spirits might be thought of as powers or extraordinary beings or occurrences that have to be attended to through ceremony or by offerings or by prayers. Even tribal Christians accept phenomenal, even miraculous, occurrences and sacred beings. Also part of the environment are places (sacred or otherwise), animals, and people. Sickness is perceived as negatively affecting everything around the individual patient. Not only that, but healing is an ongoing process. Consequently, when a healer provides medicine and a ceremony to cure an illness, he or she also restores an out-of-balance environment that may take more than one ritual or type of medicine.

Participation in ceremonies, whether designed to honor or to heal the returning veterans, confers and confirms valued status within the society. As I argued in *Strong Hearts*, combat veterans often go through "age acceleration." The warrior sees life, death, and destruction in a compressed time span and suffers what is referred to as "survivor's guilt." In short, the warrior has seen and done things in battle that few others have seen or done. But instead of viewing age acceleration or survivor's guilt as being totally negative experiences, Native societies quite often equate age with wisdom. The warrior has actually gained knowledge by experiencing the terrible consequences of combat. A Ho-Chunk elder said it best: "We honor our veterans for their bravery and because by seeing death on the battlefield, they truly know the greatness of life."[19]

Steven Silver, a psychologist, also framed the readjustment of Native Vietnam veterans in cultural terms. The tribes fought low-intensity, highly ritualized warfare usually centered on taking captives to replace deceased relatives or to serve as sacrifices to the dead person's spirit. Whatever the causes of warfare, the tribal peoples expected that their warriors would be traumatized by killing. Consequently, they developed specific ceremonies to help warriors cross the line between war and peacetime pursuits. Essentially, tribal peoples developed powerful social contracts with their warriors. The relationship between the warrior and society was balanced: the people prepared the warrior for battle and arranged to reintegrate him or her back into society with appropriate ceremonies; the warriors defended tribal boundaries, re-

WICAZO SA REVIEW

SPRING 2017

placed lost relatives with captives, and instilled in their societies a sense of pride and strength.[20]

In support of Silver's ideas, Donald Johnson and Robin LaDue argue that traditional healing involves entire communities. Warfare changes all who have seen it for the rest of their lives. Traditional Native Americans experience life as a cycle. The community, the belief system, the ceremonies, and their relationships are in a perpetual state of renewal. The traumatized warrior must be reintegrated into that cycle.[21]

A sociologist colleague, who shall be anonymous, once critiqued these studies of wartime trauma as "only a snapshot" of a social problem. He was wrong, of course, because tribal healing is continual and community based. The studies that were done, however, focused on Native American Vietnam veterans and so only encompassed one group. Given that these studies were in fact longitudinal, the snapshot critique really does not hold water. Since the recognition of PTSD as a genuine emotional disorder, various kinds of treatments have been developed to combat its effects. It is a debilitating ailment that merits compensation from the Veterans Administration at the very least. But PTSD can be the result of just about any kind of serious trauma. Rape and abuse victims, survivors of various kinds of disasters, and war veterans are all potential PTSD sufferers. In addition, American military forces have become involved in combat in Grenada, Panama, the Gulf War, and prolonged wars in Iraq and Afghanistan since these studies were undertaken. What of these Native American veterans?

CONVERSATIONS AT A GOURD DANCE

We can be relatively certain that the veterans of the wars in Iraq and Afghanistan are suffering PTSD at the same or even greater levels as veterans of the Vietnam War, simply because the Iraq and Afghanistan veterans have on average more deployments to the war zone. PTSD is apparently cumulative. It stands to reason that multiple deployments—and Iraq and Afghanistan veterans have been deployed as many as six times—simply increase the exposure to war-related trauma and raise the levels of combat-induced stress.

I was fortunate to have conversations with three Native American veterans at powwows in Arizona. At each of these events, the intertribal dances were preceded by a gourd dance. Gourd dancers usually have various military patches, badges, ribbons, and medals attached to their red and blue dance blankets. I struck up conversations with three veterans at three different powwows. One man was a veteran of the fighting in Afghanistan, and the other two had seen combat in both Afghanistan and Iraq. All three had been brought into the arena to participate by older men, only one of whom was a member of this particular young man's tribe/nation. The gourd dance itself was not a tradition of any one of their cultures. The dance and its attending ceremonies and songs were in fact introductions, showing the way diverse Native American nations have adapted traditions over time.

During casual conversations between sets of songs, they all mentioned that they had encountered problems dealing with their own readjustment after the wars in which they fought and displayed classic symptoms of PTSD: sleep intrusions, heightened startle responses, anger, depression, flashbacks, and feelings of isolation. They also expressed the opinion that, like a large percentage of Vietnam veterans I surveyed and interviewed over twenty years ago, their own tribal governments were not doing enough to ease their return from war. They also suggested that their own traditions of returning warriors from combat were either forgotten, not practiced, or too expensive to have performed. They felt, however, that their participation in the gourd dance ceremonies was helping them combat PTSD in ways that non–Native American psychological counseling, group therapy, or VA compensation could not. The three intimated that dancing with other veterans, being honored for their sacrifices by other Native people, and taking in the power invested in the traditional songs of the gourd dance all helped in their healing. It seemed that their only regret was that very few of their fellow Native veterans were joining them in any kind of Native American ceremonies.

Talking to these three men who fought in Afghanistan and Iraq cannot, of course, be taken, in the words of my dismissive colleague mentioned above, as even a "snapshot" of all Native veterans of these wars. Simply put, more study is required.[22] But one thing about our conversations stood out. The men expressed the notion that it was easier for them to talk to an older combat veteran like myself than to others who had no such experience themselves.

From my own experience, I know that it is extremely difficult to discuss the kinds of things that happen in war. The feeling that others cannot possibly understand the horrors and terror of combat or envision the destruction that modern weapons can inflict on human beings and the environment unless they have been there is strong among combat veterans. That is precisely why many relatives of combat veterans say that the veterans rarely, if ever, speak of their wartime experiences. Perhaps the younger Native veterans are not so very different from their older relatives who went to Vietnam. The ceremonies are alive and well; the veterans need to seek them out.

A U T H O R   B I O G R A P H Y

Tom Holm (Creek/Cherokee) is an emeritus professor in the American Indian studies program at the University of Arizona. His 1996 book, *Strong Hearts, Wounded Souls: Native American Veterans of the Vietnam War*, was a finalist for the Victor Turner Prize in ethnographic writing in Canada. His latest academic book, *The Great Confusion in Indian Affairs: Native Americans and Whites in the Progressive Era*, was released in 2005 by the University of Texas Press. A Cherokee / Muskogee Creek from Oklahoma, Professor Holm has served on numerous Native American boards, panels, and working groups. He is a Marine Corps veteran of the Vietnam War and has taken part in several federal programs dealing with veterans' affairs.

N O T E S

1 Tom Holm, *Strong Hearts, Wounded Souls: Native American Veterans of the Vietnam War* (Austin: University of Texas Press, 1996), 12–17.

2 See ibid., especially chapter 4; and Tom Holm, "Culture, Ceremonialism, and Stress: American Indian Veterans and the Vietnam War," *Armed Forces & Society* 12, no. 2 (Winter 1986): 241–42.

3 See Holm, *Strong Hearts, Wounded Souls*, 30–65; Holm, "Patriots and Pawns: State Use of American Indians in the Military and the Process of Nativization in the United States," in *The State of Native America: Genocide, Colonization, and Resistance*, ed. M. Annette Jaimes (Boston: Smith End Press, 1992), 354–57; Winona LaDuke, *The Militarization of Indian Country* (East Lansing: Makwa Enewed, Michigan State University Press, 2013), 3–8.

4 William C. Meadows, *Kiowa, Apache and Comanche Military Societies* (Austin: University of Texas Press, 1999), 143–61, 276–78.

5 Frank Montour, introduction to *Report of the Working Group on American Indian Vietnam Era Veterans* (Washington, D.C.: Readjustment Counseling Service, Department of Veterans Affairs, 1992), 6–7.

6 Holm, *Strong Hearts, Wounded Souls*, 169–97.

7 Tom Holm, "The Indian Veterans of the Vietnam War: Restoring Harmony through Tribal Ceremony," *Four Winds* 3 (Autumn 1982): 34–37; Holm, "Intergenerational Rapprochement among American Indians: A Study of Thirty-Five Indian Veterans of the Vietnam War," *Journal of Military and Political Sociology* 12 (Spring 1984): 161–70; Holm, "The National Survey of Vietnam Era American Indian Veterans: A Preliminary Reconnaissance," *Wicazo Sa Review* 1 (Spring 1985): 36–38; Holm, "Culture, Ceremonialism and Stress: A Study of Thirty-Five American Indian Veterans of the Vietnam War," *Armed Forces and Society* 12 (Winter 1986): 237–51; Holm, "Forgotten Warriors: American Indian Servicemen in Vietnam," *Vietnam Generation* 2 (Spring 1989): 56–68.

8 Veterans Administration Advisory Committee on Native American Veterans, *Final Report* (Washington, D.C.: Veterans Administration, February 1, 1988); Veterans Administration Advisory Committee on Native American Veterans, *Third and Final Report* (Washington, D.C.: Department of Veterans Affairs, February 1, 1989).

9 *Shadow of the Warrior: American Indian Counseling Perspectives*, produced by the Veterans Administration, 1986, https://www.youtube.com /watch?v=Cuw6frmqzJY. See also Holm, *Strong Hearts, Wounded Souls*, 13–14.

10 *Diagnostic and Statistical Manual of Mental Disorders*, 3rd ed. (Washington, D.C.: American Psychiatric Association, 1980); see also www .Comanchero.org/ptsd_diagnostic -criteria.htm for a concise list

of PTSD symptoms from the *DSM-III*.

11 Tom Holm, "The National Survey of Indian Vietnam Veterans," *American Indian and Alaska Native Mental Health Research: The Journal of the National Center* 6, no. 1 (1994): 18–28.

12 "Myths and Realities: A Study of Attitudes toward Vietnam Era Veterans," submitted by the Veterans Administration to the Committee on Veterans' Affairs, United States Senate, 96th Cong., 2nd sess. (Washington, D.C.: Government Printing Office, 1980).

13 "A History of Camp Chaparral," www.waterplanet.ws/cc/History .html.

14 Kathleen M. McNamara, "Healthcare and Issues of Racial and Ethnic Diversity," in *The Praeger Handbook of Veterans' Health: History, Challenges, Issues, and Developments, Vol. III: Mental Health Treatment and Rehabilitation*, ed. Thomas W. Miller (Santa Barbara, Calif.: Praeger, 2012), 286.

15 Ibid.

16 See "Psychological Trauma for American Indians Who Served in Vietnam," U.S. Department of Veterans' Affairs, www.ptsd .va.gov/professional/treatment /cultural/psych-trauma-native -american.asp.

17 Deborah Bassett, Debra Buch-wald, and Spero Manson, "Post Traumatic Stress Disorder among American Indians and Alaska Natives: A Review of the Literature," *Social Psychiatry and Psychiatric Epidemiology* 49, no. 3 (2014): 417–33.

18 *Report of the Working Group*, 6.

19 Holm, *Strong Hearts, Wounded Souls*, 192.

20 Steven Silver, "Lessons from Child of Water," in *Report of the Working Group*, 12–24.

21 Donald Johnson and Robin LaDue, "A Cultural and Community Process," in *Report of the Working Group*, 39–42.

22 Two available studies are Lawrence W. Gross, "Assisting American Indian Veterans of Iraq and Afghanistan Cope with Posttraumatic Stress Disorder: Lessons from Vietnam Veterans and the Writings of Jim Northrup," *American Indian Quarterly* 31, no. 3 (Summer 2007): 373–409; Elizabeth Brooks, Carol Kaufman, Herbert T. Nagamoto, Nancy K. Dailey, Byron D. Bair, and Jay Shore, "The Impact of Demographic Differences on Native Veterans' Outpatient Service Utilization," *Psychological Services* 12, no. 2 (2015): 134–40.